RISE OF THE RIGHT

Published in 2019 by Hardie Grant Books,
an imprint of Hardie Grant Publishing

Hardie Grant Books (Melbourne)
Building 1, 658 Church Street
Richmond, Victoria 3121

Hardie Grant Books (London)
5th & 6th Floors
52–54 Southwark Street
London SE1 1UN

hardiegrantbooks.com

A catalogue record for this book is available from the National Library of Australia

Rise of the Right
ISBN 978 1 74379 542 2

10 9 8 7 6 5 4 3 2 1

Cover design by Josh Durham, Design by Committee
Cover image courtesy Bigstock/ingae
Typeset in 11.5/16 pt Bembo by Cannon Typesetting
Printed by McPherson's Printing Group, Maryborough, Victoria

The paper this book is printed on is certified against the Forest Stewardship Council® Standards. FSC® promotes environmentally responsible, socially beneficial and economically viable management of the world's forests.

RISE OF THE RIGHT

THE WAR ON AUSTRALIA'S LIBERAL VALUES

GREG BARNS

Hardie Grant
BOOKS

Contents

Introduction

Since the election of John Howard as Prime Minister in 1996, the populist right has been on the rise in Australia. Howard's ascendancy and his years as Prime Minister confirmed his predecessor Paul Keating's observation that when you change Prime Ministers, you change the nation.

What do we mean by the term the 'populist right'? It is a mindset and view of the world marked by intolerance of diversity, anti-globalism, nativism, and a strong belief that the rule of law comes second to national security, including legislation that interferes markedly with the balance of power between security and liberty. Perhaps its most hideous manifestation lies in its callous indifference to the suffering of men, women and children in immigration detention because they are 'The Other'.

The soft peddling by Howard on the rise of Pauline Hanson and what she stood for, the Tampa incident, the Children

Overboard scandal and the War on Terror were all milestones in the rise of the populist right in Australia.

Over the past two decades, this has manifested itself in a myriad of ways. One that has become obvious is the redefined term 'progressive'. A telling illustration is the characterisation of the re-elected Victorian Labor government led by Daniel Andrews as progressive. Andrews, after recording a thumping win at the November 2018 election, described Victoria as 'the most progressive state in the nation'. Commentators agreed, including *The Age*'s Julie Szego, who in a column on 1 December 2018 endorsed Mr Andrews' remark and talked up the liberal nirvana that is Victoria.

Yet this is a government that is addicted to hardline law-and-order policies and punitive drug laws. This so-called progressive government has more prisoners and offenders awaiting trial than at any other time in Victoria's history. Further, the Andrews' government proudly boasts of having the toughest bail laws in the nation.

Another case of a so-called progressive's swing to the right is that of the former federal Education Minister Simon Birmingham. A federal government minister who once regarded himself as proudly liberal, he has been blocking independently and rigorously assessed funding grants for research. *The Guardian*'s Paul Karp reported on 26 October 2018 that Senate estimates 'revealed that Birmingham blocked $1.4m of discovery grants'.

The idea that government should be in the business of curtailing freedom of thought and expression after projects have passed muster with an independent expert body is a dangerously illiberal one. One assumes Birmingham acted as he did to curry favour with the populist right in the Liberal Party.

Members of the populist right consider courts a nuisance, or worse still, tools of dreaded 'social engineering'. Courts get in the way of law-and-order agendas so beloved of the right. And courts get in the way when it comes to trampling on the rights of people deemed by the populist right to not deserve rights at all.

The fact that a government appoints former police officer Peter Dutton – who is proud to see the world in simplistic terms, and who thinks it is legitimate to detain children in horrific conditions as a means of deterring people smugglers – to highly sensitive and nuanced areas of policy such as immigration and home security says much about the decline of liberal values in Australia.

Because the populist right has championed the concept of national security as a measure of control, it labels anyone who opposes the expansion of military and police powers in that context as 'soft' so that there is little demur when legislation like the ominously called Defence Amendment (Call Out of the Australian Defence Force) Bill 2018, is proposed. The Senate, with the Australian Labor Party joining the Coalition, passed the bill – which markedly expands the capacity for the military to take over our streets because there might be a 'domestic violence' situation about to erupt (such as a terrorist attack or some other form of widespread violence) – on 27 November 2018.

While the populist right likes to portray itself as standing up for the 'ordinary' people against 'elites', and likes to assert that it is persecuted and harassed by a leftist cabal that lurks within the ABC, universities and institutions like the Australian Human Rights Commission, the reality is very different. The populist right has never had it so good. It savages and bullies its opponents and has ensured that Australia leans toward being deeply conservative.

The international reputation of Australia as a nation with a poor human rights record towards asylum seekers, and as a place which thumbs its nose routinely at the United Nations, is a result of the populist right's projection of this image globally.

But the populist right's success has come at the expense of a commitment to liberal values by legislators, the media and many in the community. The ideas of tolerance and fairness, the belief in the importance of the rule of law, the fostering of diversity of cultures and beliefs, and the ideal of an open nation that embraces the world and is committed to international cooperation have all taken a beating over the past two decades.

The result is a divided and diminished Australia. We live in a nation that desperately needs to fight back against the populist right before we see the rise of dangerous nationalism, which has been embraced so comprehensively in countries like Hungary, Poland, Austria and, most recently, Italy.

Understanding the power and tactics of the populist right, taking measure of its hypocrisy and cant, and identifying the damage it is doing to a liberal democracy like Australia is essential if there is to be a sustained rallying to the cause of liberal values.

CHAPTER 1

The Decline of Liberal Values: Is Australia any Different?

To most, the notion of 'liberal values' means respect for openness, progress, tolerance and the rule of law. In Australia, however, these values are under threat. All around us we see mistreatment of asylum seekers; a focus by the media and politicians on the race of people accused or convicted of crimes; and a cavalcade of 'anti-terror' laws that crush fundamental rights, to mention just a few prominent examples of the troubling trend.

Such threats to liberal values are not just found on the fringes of our community or body politic. Two of our nation's most powerful politicians, Prime Minister Scott Morrison and Home Affairs Minister Peter Dutton, exemplify the decline of liberal values in this nation while, ironically, belonging to the conservative political force that calls itself the Liberal Party. As well, our media (print and electronic) are dominated by partisan advocates for an Australia that is decidedly illiberal.

To focus for a moment on Morrison and Dutton, the former was the architect and hectoring champion of one of the triumphs of the illiberal culture, a triumph that the Canberra Press Gallery regards as one of the great political successes of the Liberal Party and its coalition colleagues, the Nationals. The initiative, devised by Morrison in the 2013 Australian federal election and known as 'Operation Sovereign Borders', was a forerunner of a proposal by US President Donald Trump to build an impenetrable wall on the US border with Mexico. It militarised border control and allowed the use of military force to 'push back' boats of asylum seekers from Australian shores. The operation, shrouded in secrecy then and now, represents a breach of international law in two respects – firstly, in not allowing persons to make claims for asylum; and secondly, in being completely reckless in its judgement of whether it is safe to return people to the hostile waters north and west of Australia, or to the countries from which they are fleeing.

Morrison recorded a video for those poor souls detained in the Australian offshore detention centres of Manus Island and Nauru. In it he warned them: 'If you choose not to go home then you will spend a very, very long time here' – once again a breach of international law, which requires those seeking asylum to have their claims processed expeditiously and fairly. Then there was Morrison's instruction to security agencies such as the Australian Security Intelligence Organisation (ASIO) to delay security clearances for asylum seekers. According to Lenore Taylor, reporting in *The Sydney Morning Herald* on 17 February of that year, he had also, in 2011, urged his colleagues 'to capitalise on the electorate's growing concerns about "Muslim immigration", "Muslims in Australia" and the "inability of Muslim migrants to integrate"'.

It was a former Australian prime minister, John Howard – a mentor and political hero of Morrison's – who determinedly worked not only to dismantle liberal values in Australia but to legitimise the voices of prejudice and irrationality. In fact, the erosion and dismantling of the liberal values consensus can be traced to the very early days of Howard's time in office – as will be discussed in detail. But while Morrison is deeply conservative and decidedly illiberal when it comes to immigration and social issues generally (for example, he opposed the legalisation of marriage for same-sex couples), he is at least more accommodating of the idea of open markets and is apparently opposed to the zero-sum game of international trade.[1]

Dutton, on the other hand, is straight out of the 'insurgent right' – a term coined by Malcolm Turnbull in his tumultuous dying days as Australian prime minister. It is the force within politics and the media today that aggressively pushes a vision of authoritarian illiberal democracy. Like US President Donald Trump, Peter Dutton is contemptuous of the two important checks on abuse of power in a democracy: the judiciary and the media, both of which often oppose, or at least question, the government of the day. (About the latter he said that the ABC and *The Guardian,* among other media outlets he regards as hostile, were 'dead to me'.) Dutton is the man who has zealously prosecuted a cruel, and internationally condemned, suite of measures against asylum seekers, both onshore and offshore; who whips up fears about Sudanese youth in Melbourne; who, on economic matters, has been unashamedly populist (right wing but championing anti-elitist sentiments) while peddling the (anti-immigrant) nativist argument that migration costs jobs; who peddles monocultural rhetoric ('speak English or leave') towards migrants, but who, on the other hand, bemused and horrified the South African government with his invitation to white farmers from that country to resettle in Australia; and who refused to be part of the National Apology to the Stolen Generations that united politicians across the spectrum in 2007. And this is by no means a complete list of Dutton's illiberal sentiments and conduct.

Once, Dutton would have been an outcast in the Liberal Party, a man thought to be too dangerous and extreme to promote to high office. But now, he and his colleagues who share his black-and-white vision have the Liberal Party by the throat. They run the show. While there was some relief that Dutton's pitch for the leadership of the Liberal Party in August 2018 did not bear fruit, that does not mean that he and his somewhat cleverer and subtler counterparts, like Prime Minister Scott Morrison, are not equally wedded to shredding liberal values.

In fact, as a consequence of the Howard and post Howard era, the party that Robert Menzies created in 1944 has become so illiberal that describing true liberalism requires one to call it 'small l'. And the decline of liberal values is not confined to the party that takes its name; the Australian Labor Party (ALP) has been equally culpable in this state of affairs. In the case of the ALP, it is as though being seen to be liberal is to invite excoriating attacks from the most voluble media in which one is deemed to be 'soft' or 'extreme'. Among the 'voluble media' are the Murdoch media outlets, both print and the increasingly influential TV channel Sky News, as well as radio shows hosted by prominent Sydney personalities and television programs like Channel 7's *Sunday Night*. These are the champions of the authoritarian 'them versus us' and simplistic black-versus-white rhetoric and imagery.

But let's take a step back.

Liberal values?

What do we mean by 'liberal values'? Firstly, let's establish what we *don't* mean, because both the idea and the term 'liberal values', so beloved by politicians, has got itself a bad rap in recent times.

Particularly in the past two decades, this term has famously been used by world leaders to justify military interventions. While he was prime minister of the United Kingdom, Tony Blair – like Australia's John Howard, an enthusiastic supporter of the US Bush administration's disastrous wars in Iraq and Afghanistan – was a signed-up member of the 'liberal values' club when it came to justifying wars. Arguing the case for military coalitions in global trouble spots – in the case of these comments, Kosovo – Blair said that the actions of such a coalition were 'guided by a more subtle blend of mutual self-interest and moral purpose in defending the values we cherish. In the end, values and interests merge'.[2] Blair's notion of liberal values seems valid, but the context is highly problematic, as recent history shows us.

And then there is the critique of some on the populist left that the term 'liberal values' connotes an upholding of privilege or is simply what underpins economic 'neo-liberalism'.

As expressed by American writer and political commentator Jonathan Chait:

> The Marxist left has always dismissed liberalism's commitment to protecting the rights of its political opponents – you know, the old line often misattributed to Voltaire, 'I disapprove of what you have to say, but I'll defend to the death your right to say it' – as hopelessly naïve. If you maintain equal political rights for the oppressive capitalists and their proletarian victims, this will simply keep in place society's unequal power relations. Why respect the rights of the class whose power you're trying to smash? And so, according to Marxist thinking, your political rights depend entirely on what class you belong to. The modern far left has borrowed the Marxist critique of liberalism and substituted race and gender identities for economic ones.[3]

To be clear, this book is not a defence of liberal values as a useful tool for international military or regime destabilisation; nor is it about seeing liberal values in the context of maintaining and bolstering inequality. Instead, it seeks to argue that liberal values, in the Australian context, are overwhelmingly positive and restoring them to our body politic and broader community is a necessity if we do not want to continue on the road to a fearful, narrow and divided future.

Liberal values in the Australian context

Perhaps not surprisingly, but certainly ironically given the subject matter of this book, a Google search of 'liberal values in

Australia' results in pages of links to Liberal Party websites. Yet what we are focussing on are the core, universal liberal values to which Australia ought to subscribe, given it claims to be a liberal democracy.

There is no better enunciation of liberal values in the context of these times than the one recently described by the London-based newspaper *The Economist*. Throughout its 175 years, the paper has consistently championed social and economic liberalism, and so concerned is it by the rise of illiberal democracy and populism that it has recently embarked on a campaign to defend liberal values. In a lengthy essay published on 12 June 2018, its Bagehot column set out the key elements of liberal values that remain highly relevant today. 'The central idea of liberalism is the primacy of the individual rather than the collective,' the column notes. Then there is civic respect, a belief in progress, and a distrust of power.

We might also look at the Museum of Australian Democracy based in Canberra. It says that:

> Australian democracy has, at its heart, the following core defining values: freedom of election and being elected; freedom of assembly and political participation; freedom of speech, expression and religious belief; rule of law; and other basic human rights.[4]

To these definitions and description we can add that liberal values in the Australian context, and in fact in the broader context of liberal democracies generally, mean a commitment to free trade; an open society that includes a compassionate and liberal migration program; and a commitment to continue to tread the path of globalisation while ensuring that its benefits are better shared. In this regard, one might see German Chancellor Angela Merkel as an exemplar of liberal values, as opposed to her counterparts in Italy and Poland or even the United Kingdom in its post-Brexit haze. Or for another analogy, Canadian Prime Minister Justin Trudeau.

Up until the era of Howard's prime ministership, the commitment to, and practice of, these liberal values in the Australian body politic had been essentially a bipartisan matter. In the time since Robert Menzies departed the scene in 1965 and since Gough Whitlam modernised the ALP from the late 1960s onwards, both the major political forces in Australia backed liberal values, more or less.

Prime ministers from Whitlam through to early Howard (pre Tampa), and their opposite numbers such as former Liberal leaders Andrew Peacock and John Hewson, were all committed to the outward-looking, globalised and domestic liberalising of Australian life. Under them, Australia became a global citizen, signing up to a raft of treaties and agreements that bespoke liberal values, while at home those instruments were given effect in domestic laws such as the *Racial Discrimination Act* and the *Sex Discrimination Act* and through a liberal policy approach.

Since the early efforts of the Whitlam (Labor) Government, and strengthened by Liberal Prime Minister Malcolm Fraser (a small-l liberal), multiculturalism and an aversion to a return to the dark days of race-tainted politics (the White Australia Policy, for example) were a matter of fact. When Howard, in his first stint as Liberal Party leader (1985–1989) complained about the level of Asian immigration in 1988, members of the Liberal Party crossed the floor of the federal parliament to oppose him. His comments were not even lauded by hard-right commentators or headline writers.

As writer David Marr noted in *The Sydney Morning Herald* on 23 March 2017, Howard

> had not anticipated the wave of disgust that swept the country as he brought race politics to Canberra. Liberal voters were appalled. The liberal press was brutal. Shadow ministers crossed the floor to repudiate his shift in direction. He became a figure of ridicule, even contempt. Within months, Andrew Peacock was once again Opposition leader; Howard would spend the next six years plotting to get his old job back.

Thirty years on, Howard's comments are mild compared with what is said and published in reference to members of the Sudanese community, Muslims and other minority groups by 'shock jock' broadcasters like 2GB Sydney's Ray Hadley and Alan Jones, and by newspapers such as News Corp's *Herald Sun* and *The Daily Telegraph*, their front pages generally alarmist and divisive, with their columnists (including Andrew Bolt, Miranda Devine, Paul Murray and Rita Panahi) attracting large audiences not only for their print appearances but through the powerful medium of Sky News. The difference is that, today, leaders who play the race card are lauded by key sections of the electorate, and politicians clamber aboard to fuel the illiberal fire.

While the decline of liberal values in Australia can indeed be traced to the government that Howard led from 1996 to 2007, some might say it should more specifically be traced to the tacit approval, by Howard and his government, of the rhetoric of the then newly minted Independent Member for the Queensland seat of Oxley, Pauline Hanson; by the infamous 2001 Tampa incident; and by the Australian Government's response to the events of 9/11 in the United States of America.

There has been no effective turning back of the tide since the Howard years. In the same way as the former UK prime minister and the UK Labour Party effectively embraced the neoliberal economic agenda of the conservative Margaret Thatcher, who led the United Kingdom from 1979 until 1991, the Rudd and Gillard governments made no sustained attempt to restore the liberal consensus that had existed before Howard began to rip it apart in 1996. Tellingly, a Rudd commitment to enshrine human rights into law in the form of a Human Rights Act or charter was shelved early in his premiership. And in his desperate attempt to win another term for the ALP and himself after he deposed Julia Gillard in 2013, Rudd embarked on a shameful exercise in neocolonialism by doling out billions of dollars to impoverished Papua New Guinea and Nauru in an attempt to convince voters he could 'stop the boats'.

Within the Liberal Party, former prime minister Tony Abbott (himself a self-confessed hard-right Anglophile), Dutton, Morrison and outspoken backbench MPs like the former soldier Andrew Hastie have all accelerated the decline of liberal values in a marked fashion. They have done so with little or no opposition from those in the Liberal Party who regard themselves ideologically as more liberal than conservative. While, even in the years of Howard, a handful of Liberal MPs such as Petro Georgiou, Judi Moylan and Judith Troeth would speak out about the shame of the detention of asylum seekers, and in particular children, there has been no public or even private opposition since they left the national scene a decade ago. And in the ALP as well, there is silence on this issue; their policy settings when they were in office from 2007 to 2013 were only slightly more compassionate. This from an allegedly progressive political force, and certainly one that in the past had espoused and practised liberal values (think the Whitlam Government and landmark anti-discrimination laws of the Hawke Government).

While this book is not about asylum seekers – much has been written on this topic, mostly revealing the horror of the regime – the matter of how legislators and government treat human beings is emblematic of whether liberal values are being eroded or indeed altogether ignored within a nation. But it is not only on the issue of asylum seekers that the ALP is guilty of joining in the assault on liberal values. Rarely does Labor oppose the attacks on courts and the rule of law that individuals like Dutton and his allies launch with astonishing regularity. The party seems easily cowed by the tabloid media, abetted by its slavish devotion to marginal seat opinion polling numbers. In fact, the ALP is sometimes happy to join in the assault on liberal values. Victorian Premier Daniel Andrews – generally regarded, believe it or not, as a progressive leader – has regularly joined in the attacks on his state's judiciary made by Dutton and others, and his recently re-elected government has stripped fundamental rights from defendants in criminal proceedings. Andrews and his government jump to the dissonant tune of Melbourne's *Herald Sun*, a highly influential illiberal and authoritarian force in Victoria.

On 24 May 2018, the then New South Wales ALP leader, Luke Foley, scored himself a headline in *The Daily Telegraph* – which, in its world view and outlook, is a carbon copy of the *Herald Sun* (or vice versa, take your pick) – by bemoaning what he called the flight of white Anglo-European families ('white flight'!) from parts of Western Sydney because these areas were being overrun by Iraqi and Syrian refugees.

The rise and rise of the heirs of Howard – epitomised in Scott Morrison and Peter Dutton and what they represent – poses a challenge to those who believe in a liberal Australia. That is, an Australia that is open, tolerant and progressive and one that values the rule of law both domestically and internationally.

The global context

The threat to liberal values in Australia can be, and must be, placed within a global setting because the rhetoric and actions of Australia's political class, media and broader community can be seen as belonging to the trend of populist nativism that is proving potent in countries such as Poland, Hungary, the Czech Republic and Italy.

The potency of this force was recently and neatly summarised by the former editor of *Le Monde*, Sylvie Kauffmann, in

The New York Times on 22 September 2017. She described the emergence of

> an illiberal axis embodied by President Trump in the United States and by two leaders in Central Europe: Jaroslaw Kaczynski, the head of Poland's ruling nationalist Law and Justice party, and Prime Minister Viktor Orbán of Hungary. This axis has gone on the offensive against migrants, open borders, multiculturalism and multilateralism. What only a year ago still looked like a risky swerve from a deeply ingrained democratic culture, or a knee-jerk reaction to the omnipresence of 'political correctness,' now appears to be a joint, methodical, determined effort to undermine pillars of the liberal order and install a different set of values.

Since publication of Kauffmann's piece, Italy and the Czech Republic have elected nativist, populist governments. And as *Financial Times* journalist Edward Luce has observed, the line between illiberal democracy and autocracy is a fine one.[5]

The shift away from an open society built on liberal values is borne out by gestures such as US President Donald Trump's obsession with building a gargantuan wall along the US border with Mexico; Europe's turning its back on thousands of homeless people from Syria, Libya and other African countries by shunting them into wretched camps where men, women and children freeze in subarctic conditions and are exposed to the beating sun of high summer; the United Kingdom's spurning of Europe; the Italian Government's strident rhetoric towards asylum seekers; and the protectionist trade war being pursued by the US White House. These are all portents of the most dangerous shift in the Western world since the 1930s, when the enemies of liberal values seized control of nations such as Germany, Italy and Spain.

One of the primary architects and espousers of the nativist right is US multimillionaire Steve Bannon. The owner of Breitbart News, a nativist right-wing news site, he was President Trump's right-hand man during the 2016 election campaign until he left the White House after losing influence with the most capricious occupant of the world's most powerful political office in modern history. As the online news site Vox said of Bannon on 25 July 2018, he 'sees the world in broadly ideological terms, positioning a pro-migration and pro-trade elite against a global middle class that believes deeply in the virtues of nationalism'.

It is not an exaggeration to say that, globally, the open society built on liberal values after the horrors of World War II is teetering, as once again humankind confirms that too many of us cannot remember the past and are condemned to repeat it (to paraphrase the incisive words of the Spanish writer and philosopher George Santayana).

In 1945 another philosopher, Karl Popper, exiled from his native Europe to New Zealand, published his book *The Open Society and Its Enemies*. In one of the most extraordinary philosophical statements of the last hundred years, Popper identified that his purpose was to show

> the transition from the tribal or 'closed society,' with its submission to magical forces, to the 'open society' which sets free the critical powers of man. It attempts to show that

> the shock of this transition is one of the factors that have made possible the rise of those reactionary movements which have tried, and still try, to overthrow civilization and to return to tribalism.[6]

He was of course talking about the rise of Fascism and Communism in Europe and the closing of borders to humanity and trade.

Popper identified that humankind has an innate desire to be closed to those who do not belong to the 'tribe'. Tribalism is the enemy of civilisation because it abandons reason and critical thought for prejudice and fantasy. President Trump is as much an enemy of the open society as neo-fascists like France's Marine Le Pen and the extreme-right political forces that are emerging in Germany. In all cases, lies and fantasy are peddled by leaders and believed by their gullible supporters. Climate change is a conspiracy, trade barriers will create jobs and wealth, and migration takes local jobs and destroys the social fabric of society. These are all lies but they placate the fearful and insecure.

It is worth comparing where we are today with the status quo of the 1930s, the decade when the open society was under existential threat. The tribalism of the far right is as virulent today as it was in the 1930s. Then it was the Jewish people who were scapegoated; now it is Muslims. Trade wars, protectionism, and harassment and persecution of the so-called 'elites' were dominant in the 1930s. The open liberal world order spawned by US President Woodrow Wilson and the Treaty of Versailles after World War I was collapsing.

While the rise of the extreme right in the 1930s of course resulted in the genocide of the Jewish people by the Nazis, and therefore one must be circumspect and cautious in drawing a link between then and now, there are serious consequences for the world if the populist right continues to erode open borders, free trade, multiculturalism and values like tolerance. There is no security in tribalism. The Trumps, and other political and community forces like Steve Bannon, the Brexiteers, and the boisterous media that are peddling simplistic and angry illiberal solutions and speech are the enemies of human progress.

The Economist recently issued a clarion call for the open society to be reinvigorated. 'The danger is that a rising sense of insecurity will lead to more electoral victories for closed-world types. This is the gravest risk to the free world since communism. Nothing matters more than countering it,' opined the newspaper on 30 July 2016.

Back to Australia

In Australia, the nativist and populist forces are readily apparent. In fact, despite claims to the contrary, the sorts of themes about which Sylvie Kauffmann writes are dominant in what passes for media discourse in this country. Not a week goes by without calls to substantially curtail immigration, without newspaper stories such as one in the *Herald Sun* on 10 August 2018 describing the arrest of some youth by noting 'they were of African, Asian and Middle Eastern backgrounds'. Attempts to deal with misogyny, racial discrimination and other forms of discrimination are labelled by conservative commentators and politicians as exercises in 'political correctness'.

Australian democracy, in the narrow sense of this nation being one where there is a right to vote, is not under threat, yet those other components necessary to a liberal democracy – such as genuinely independent public broadcasters, and respect for human rights and the rule of law – are vulnerable and today are threatened. It was actually one of Morrison and Dutton's former colleagues, George Brandis (now the Australian High Commissioner to London), who, in his valedictory speech to the Senate on 7 February 2018, warned that 'belligerent, intolerant populism' was on the rise in Australia.

The undermining of Australia's consensus on liberal values first occurred when Howard and his Liberal Party refused to condemn Pauline Hanson's 1996 maiden speech. Hanson railed against Indigenous Australians, immigration and multiculturalism and bemoaned the loss of businesses because, as she put it, industry protection was being dismantled. Howard's predecessors Malcolm Fraser, Bob Hawke and Paul Keating would have uncompromisingly condemned this rant, but Howard did no such thing. He sought to empathise with Hanson's supporters by suggesting he could understand why they had such views. Howard had used a tool from the hard right's armoury, which it wields when wanting to tacitly approve a concept or comment that is dripping with prejudice. The shackles of 'political correctness' were being broken in Howard's 'relaxed and comfortable' Australia. That Hanson was cataloguing a list of complaints common to the illiberal democracy brigade did not worry him, given that he agreed with much of their agenda.

But it was the Tampa incident that broke the consensus on liberal values once and for all. The history is well known.

Howard and his government – in terms of polling, on the ropes with an election on the horizon – decided to make an example of the merchant ship *Tampa*, which had, in accordance with maritime law and because its captain, Arne Rinnan, was a man of decency, picked up 433 asylum seekers, many very unwell, and headed towards the Australian territory of Christmas Island in the Indian Ocean.

The conduct of the Howard Government itself was highly authoritarian. Ignoring the welfare of the asylum seekers, it breached well-known, time-honoured law and convention by ordering Captain Rinnan not to continue his journey to Christmas Island. He rightly ignored this unlawful request and the result was the introduction of legislation that suspended the rule of law so that the military could storm the ship and ensure it did not reach Australian waters. From this emerged Howard's 'Pacific Solution' – the buying-off of impoverished countries like Papua New Guinea and Nauru where asylum seekers would be detained. As mentioned, the ALP under Kevin Rudd revisited this shame in 2013.

The Tampa incident reversed the Liberal Party's fortune – overnight adding 10 per cent to the Coalition's vote, according to former Labor strategist Geoff Walsh. One former Labor staffer says that it was as though a lid had been pulled off a large can of xenophobia, racism and nationalist fervour.

The importance of the Tampa incident in plotting the decline of liberal values is self-evident. Australia had deliberately abandoned its obligations under international law. The Howard Government was prepared to draft and introduce legislation that effectively absolved armed forces of any otherwise criminal acts they might commit in relation to the ship's crew and the desperate asylum seekers on board. Because the actions were so popular, they emboldened Howard to make border control a centrepiece of the 2001 federal election and, in the course of that campaign, to concoct the so-called 'Children Overboard' affair in which the Howard Government misled the community about ambiguous photographs showing children in the arms of their parents and other adults. Despite military advice that the photographs did not show children being thrown into the sea by their parents, the images were used during the election to demonise asylum seekers. This was an early case of one of the features of illiberal democracy – 'fake news' or 'post-truth politics'.

But tapping into the fearful, xenophobic underbelly of the Australian community worked – and it still works today. When it came to asylum seekers, the ALP gave up standing firm on liberal values. While it opposed the Tampa legislation, the Labor Party subsequently joined the Liberals in passing legislation that undermined the rule of law by allowing for detention without end for men, women and children. For those who failed to convince the executive arm of government about the merits of their claim for asylum, the laws stripped them of the right to take their case to the courts; and other laws weakened Australia's international obligations under various United Nations conventions and treaties on refugees. Goodbye open and compassionate society.

The year 2001 is, of course, synonymous with another tragedy of real significance in the story of the decline of liberal values in Australia. It was the horrific events of the 11th of

September that year, generally known as 9/11, when terrorism came to the USA in the form of a series of attacks on iconic landmarks such as New York's Twin Towers and the Pentagon.

The spawning of anti-terror laws, based in part on emergency decrees passed by the US Congress and called the Patriot Act, garnered bipartisan support in Australia. A suite of laws passed then and in the years since – over seventy in total – has truncated fundamental rights such as the right to legal counsel, open justice and detention without charge. But coupled with that has been the routine pillorying of Muslim Australians by tabloid media and politicians. After 9/11 it became fashionable to indulge in attacks on Australians who came from the Middle East (not Israel, of course) and to believe that this nation had a 'problem' with Muslims and migration. Multiculturalism and the celebration of religious and cultural diversity were to blame.

The gloves-off approach to Muslims by conservative politicians and their media allies has established a modus operandi that garners votes in parts of this nation. The caravan has moved on to Sudanese or 'African' young men who are allegedly linked to terrifying gangs that have made Melbourne so unsafe that some residents are too scared to go out at night – or at least this is what that arch practitioner of illiberalism, Dutton, tells us.

As mentioned, the seeds of the toxic weeds that are strangling liberal values in Australia were sown by John Howard and the Liberal Party that he led for twelve years. The electoral success he enjoyed over the course of those years has cowed not only the liberal wing of his own party but also the more progressive wing of the ALP. As well as Morrison and Dutton, it has created and emboldened other senior members of the Liberal Party today. One powerful and depressing testament to the decline of liberal values was the spectacle in 2017 of three senior members of Malcolm Turnbull's government – Michael Sukkar, Greg Hunt and Alan Tudge – having to apologise to the Victorian Court of Appeal for comments they made about that court's sentencing in terrorism cases while the case was still before the court.

Just as the enemies and threats to liberal values are found in the Australian media, so too is the greatest champion of those values, the ABC – making the national broadcaster one of the obsessions of the nativist right. Granted, the ABC is decidedly liberal – that is, it stands for the values of openness, progress, the exchange of ideas and a belief in rational science – but this is interpreted by the nativist right as 'left wing' or, even more extremely, 'Marxist'.

Monitoring the ABC is a full-time job for some in the Murdoch media as it pressures Canberra to take action against journalists and programs for pointing out human rights abuses or for giving a platform to despised elites such as the former human rights commissioner, Gillian Triggs. In January 2014, former prime minister Tony Abbott chided the ABC because it apparently 'dismays Australians when the national broadcaster appears to take everybody's side but our own'.

But it is not only the ABC that is subjected to the hostile rhetoric of the populist right; it is also those Australians who dare to stand against the orthodoxy of reactive conservatism. Professor Triggs is one, but Fairfax Media, the publishers of the Melbourne *Age* and *The Sydney Morning Herald*, is another. *The*

Australian, in particular, runs 'fatwas' on those in public life it sees as being treacherous to the view of Australia as a paradise of fairness. It trawled through Professor Triggs's comments as part of its campaign to bring her and the Australian Human Rights Commission to heel. The hounding by politicians of the illiberal persuasion and by the Murdoch media of a young Muslim woman then appearing on ABC television, Yassmin Abdel-Magied, for daring to tweet on Anzac Day 2017 about the injustices to asylum seekers and Palestinians, was a powerful testament to how the core liberal values of tolerance and diversity have been diminished in Australia today.

Anzac Day, 25 April, has become a highly nationalistic and even a nativist occasion, as is Australia Day, 26 January. Both days took an ugly turn courtesy of Howard, and they are now so 'sacred' that any person who fails to revere the conservative narrative surrounding them is outed and shamed by conservative media and politicians.

To those who think of Australia as a highly successful democracy whose diverse society is built on respect for liberal values, a proposition that all of this is at risk might seem alarmist. But the history of the past two decades in this country's socio-political narrative, and now the global trend towards isolation, nativism and authoritarianism, ought at least to raise the question as to whether the foundations of Australian liberal democracy are sufficiently secure to make us immune to threats from without and within.

There is nothing axiomatic about the proposition that Australia will always be a democracy. While it is not suggested that this nation is currently heading for a dictatorship, what *is* on the horizon is the prospect that, with the decline of liberal values, what is cemented is an illiberal democracy – a society in which there is a right to vote and in which politicians are accountable through the parliament but which, in other respects, seeks to police conduct to ensure that there is a 'them versus us' culture. Any individual or group that threatens this type of orthodoxy is perceived as a threat to the community. This is a paternalist democracy. Such a prospect is not an unrealistic one and, given that Australia too often is infected by global trends, particularly those that take root in the USA and Europe, it is real.

CHAPTER 2

Tracing the Decline: Hanson, Tampa and 9/11

Australia is rarely immune from events in other continents and nations but some significant factors in the nation's own political history seem to have helped to propel Australia towards an eventually illiberal stance. Among them, as we have seen, was former prime minister John Howard's response to Pauline Hanson when she first appeared on the political horizon in 1996. Then, all at once in 2001, came Tampa, the allied Children Overboard event, and 9/11.

Responding to Hanson's attack on liberal values

In political terms 1996 is a lifetime (and more) ago, but it was an important year for liberal values in Australia. It was the year that saw the election to federal parliament of Pauline Hanson, an independent candidate in the Queensland seat of Oxley, which takes in the hard-scrabble town of Ipswich and surrounds in the state's south-east.

Ironically, given subsequent events, Hanson had been disendorsed by the Liberal Party because of the contents of a letter she sent to a local newspaper when she was the Liberal candidate in the 1996 election (a poll saw John Howard and the Liberal–National coalition return to the Treasury benches for the first time since 1983).

Hanson's letter to *The Queensland Times*, published on 6 January and since forgotten by most, proved to be the lightning rod for all that has subsequently happened to her. In the letter, Hanson complained that she 'would be the first to admit that, not that many years ago the Aborigines [sic] were treated wrongly but in trying to correct this [politicians] have gone too far.' 'I don't feel responsible for the treatment of Aboriginal people in the past because I had no say but my concern now is for the future,' she wrote. And then this:

> How can you expect this race to help themselves when government showers them with money, facilities and opportunities that only these people can obtain no matter how minute the indigenous blood that is flowing through their veins, and this is what is causing racism.

Yet, when Howard was elected, he echoed her sentiments in part. In 2000 he told ABC TV's current affairs program *The 7.30 Report*:

> I speak for the entire government on this, and it's a matter that's been discussed at great length. We don't think it's appropriate for the current generation of Australians to apologise for the injustices committed by past generations.

Nevertheless, it is Howard's response to Hanson's first speech to parliament in 1996 that is arguably an early pivotal moment in the values decline traced by this book. Once again, this is a speech that, at the time, not only caused outrage and uproar but also unleashed and gave voice to what might be termed white resentment politics. But again, it seems forgotten today, because the cultural phenomenon of Pauline Hanson is now so embedded in the Australian political and public psyche.

Hanson's first speech to the House of Representatives, on 10 September 1996, could have been written today – more than two decades on – by Steve Bannon or one of the European nativists. Its theme is one of dispossession: the Anglo-European way of life is under threat; working-class whites are being discriminated against by government. Held up as scapegoats were iconic examples of liberal values – such as multiculturalism, redressing the historic and current injustices to Indigenous Australians through land rights reform, the *Family Law Act*, immigration, foreign aid, and open markets. Hanson even quoted approvingly the racist cant of the former Labor leader Arthur Calwell, who once said,

> Japan, India, Burma, Ceylon and every new African nation are fiercely anti-white and anti one another. Do we want or need any of these people here? I am one red-blooded Australian who says no and who speaks for 90% of Australians.[1]

Hanson's speech was a typical nativist speech: simplistic, bereft of analysis and empirical data – and angry. What was more significant, though, was the fact that Howard as prime minister bothered to reply to a neophyte backbencher who had been dumped as a candidate by his own party. Instead of a no *ifs* or *buts*–type response to Hanson's diatribe and trashing of the liberal agenda, Howard sought to court her voters and at the same time ignore Hanson. Journalist Michael Gawenda, writing in *The Age* on 28 October 1996, gave Howard the benefit of the doubt as to whether he supported Hanson's views, but noted that the then prime minister 'nevertheless has more empathy for those people who share them than for those who strongly reject them'. 'While he has been absolutely determined not to directly tackle the Hanson agenda,' wrote Gawenda, 'he has, more than once, made it clear that he understands why she has a following.'

An illustration of the accuracy of this insight came in an answer to a question Hanson put to Howard in parliament on 28 October 1996. Asked whether he would cut Australia's foreign aid budget so the money could be used for civil construction and national service, Howard answered unequivocally in one sense. He upheld the idea of foreign aid and the level of it at the time. But equally he was at pains to point out, in what was a relatively short answer, that he could 'understand the feelings of Australians who think that their taxes are wasted in relation to aid to those countries' and that he could 'understand why, in times of difficulty – in particular, in areas of economic and social difficulty in Australia – some Australians would look suspiciously upon the provision of foreign aid' and that he thought Hanson had raised 'an important question', and that she of course was 'entitled, like any other honourable member, to ask questions in this parliament, and [he would] endeavour to answer it as comprehensively as [he could]'. This was a clever response by Howard because, while it defended the government's position, it sent a clear message to Hanson and Howard supporters that this prime minister was somewhat sympathetic with their position, and that he would not ignore them or even seek to set them right about their views.

Hanson of course fitted within the broader project of Howard's promise that he believed a pall of 'political correctness' had been cast over public discourse in Australia before he assumed office in 1996 but that he wanted a 'relaxed and comfortable' nation where people like Hanson and those who supported her illiberal and nativist sentiments could feel free to speak without fear of reprisal.

The fact that Hanson's every utterance, including her first speech, was being writ large in broadcasts and newspapers across the nation was damaging to cohesion in Australian society, and its reputation internationally seemed less important to Howard than his cynical strategy of using Hanson's extremism for support in political terms. It suited his failure to uphold social, as opposed to economic, liberal values.

Ten years on, Howard was still defending his failure to confront Hanson. As she rose again and found herself elected as a Queensland senator in 2016, Hanson produced another stock-in-trade nativist first speech. This time Asians had been replaced by Muslims as the existential threat to Anglo-European Australia. At a media conference in July that year, responding as former prime minister to the question of whether Hanson would be an unwelcome presence in the next parliament, Howard defended his decade-old approach to her:

> I didn't agree with her when she said we were being flooded by Asians because we weren't, and I didn't agree with her when she said that Aboriginal people weren't amongst the most disadvantaged in our community because those things were manifestly wrong.

But it needed to be remembered, he said, that Hanson was 'articulating the concerns of people who felt left out'. And to attack Hanson was then, and is now, a mistake, according to Howard, because the more she was attacked, 'the more popular she became because those attacks enhanced her Australian battler image and she plays off that'.[2] At least Howard has been consistent in his approach to Pauline Hanson and what she represents. But, given the way he responded to her in 1996, his strategy of not giving her airplay appears more a wish than a reality.

Howard's failure was, and remains to this day, that he did not make a full rebuttal of Hanson's dangerous, divisive rhetoric. To say people vote for her and support her views is to say that he, as a leader, had no business in seeking to stand unambiguously for liberal values, particularly social liberalism. Instead he would, and did, pander to the nativist and reactionary toxicity that Hanson and her supporters represented and still represent today. As the Australian correspondent for *The Economist* noted on 11 June 1998:

> Mr Howard has made a hash of his response to Mrs Hanson. In 1996 he ignored calls even from his own supporters to repudiate her racial views. He argued it would give her more

publicity than she deserved. This approach backfired. Mrs Hanson recently described Mr Howard as a 'gentleman'.

As well she might have done.

Tampa

The capacity and willingness of Howard and his government to provide succour to the nativist cause and again drive a stake into the heart of liberal values were amply demonstrated courtesy of that ship that was sailing towards Christmas Island in August 2001.

The Tampa incident is now the stuff of history, with the National Museum of Australia's website carrying this neat summary of the events, the impact of which is still sadly with us today:

> On 24 August 2001, the *Palapa*, a small Indonesian fishing boat overloaded with 433 mainly Hazara asylum-seekers from Afghanistan, became stranded in international waters about 140 kilometres north of Christmas Island. The asylum-seekers were rescued by the Norwegian container ship, the MV *Tampa*, under direction by the Australian Maritime Safety Authority.
>
> The *Tampa*'s captain, Arne Rinnan, then set course for the Indonesian city of Merak, the closest port with facilities to dock such a large vessel. However, some of those rescued threatened to commit suicide if they were returned to Indonesia; others entered the ship's bridge, and told Rinnan to take them to Christmas Island.

However, the Australian Government refused to allow the *Tampa* to land any of the asylum-seekers. Prime Minister John Howard said, 'I believe it is in Australia's national interest that we draw a line on what is increasingly becoming an uncontrollable number of illegal arrivals in this country.'

Many of the asylum-seekers on board the ship were in poor health. Over 48 hours, Rinnan made repeated requests to Australian authorities for assistance. These requests were acknowledged but not acted on, so Rinnan decided to enter Australian waters.

The ship crossed the Australian maritime boundary on 29 August, shortly before midday. Australian authorities advised Rinnan that he was in 'flagrant breach' of the law, and the Government dispatched 45 Special Air Service (SAS) troops to board the ship and prevent it from sailing any closer to Christmas Island.[3]

It was no coincidence that Howard was facing an election later in 2001 and had lost a previously safe Liberal seat in Brisbane earlier in the year. The hostile response by the Howard Government to the *Tampa*'s plea for humanity on the part of the Australian Government was immensely popular, and Howard and his government were re-elected for a third term.

Apart from the politics of the Tampa incident, the trashing of liberal values was deeply disturbing. We can start with the undermining of the rule of law. As the great philosopher of liberalism John Locke put it, 'Where-ever law ends, tyranny begins.' This was an apt description of the Howard Government's urgently drafted Border Protection Bill 2001. The bill was presented to the parliament by Howard and sponsored by his Immigration minister, Philip Ruddock, an erstwhile Liberal. The bill allowed Australian military personnel to board the *Tampa* and use force to remove it from Australian territorial seas. It gave the military carte blanche to commit criminal offences, and civil wrongs such as assault, and it did so by removing any liability under criminal or civil law. There was no judicial oversight and there were no consequences for wrongdoing. In other words, it created a law-free zone on the *Tampa*. In blatant disregard for Australia's obligations under international and domestic migration laws, the bill stated that no person would be assessed to see if they fitted the criteria for refugee status.

In what was to be, with hindsight, one of the last occasions on which the ALP would stand firm against attacks on the rule of law, its leader, Kim Beazley, rightly observed that the bill meant that

> no matter what the circumstances, it will be a reasonable and authoritative thing for an Australian officer to take a boat that is sinking, and in which there are life threatening situations involving the people on board, and order it out. That will be capable of being sustained by this bill – drag the boat out, sink it, people die. It does not matter what you think ought to happen; that is what this bill permits.[4]

The Howard Government's response to Tampa also undermined another important liberal value: that of a nation complying with its international law obligations, in this case both the Law of the Sea and the Refugee Convention. In respect of the former, international maritime law expert Don Rothwell from the Australian National University said in June 2002 that

> Australia's response to the Tampa incident in law of the sea terms is difficult to justify, especially given Australia's central role in that event. The … acts of closing the territorial sea and refusing entry, failing to respond to a ship in distress, and using military forces against a merchant ship to protect Australia's sovereign rights are unprecedented.[5]

As the University of New South Wales's Professor Martin Krygier would observe in 2015, the prime enemy and target of the rule of law is 'arbitrary power [because it] threatens the freedom, dignity and security of the lives of all who are subject to it'.[6]

The *Tampa*'s captain and crew, and the 433 desperate individuals to whom they had provided shelter and safety, were simply disregarded in the Howard Government's extraordinary exercise in the abuse of power. This legislation was the stuff of an authoritarian regime, not of a government purporting to uphold liberal values, and in particular the rule of law.

For Prime Minister Howard, the Tampa incident was a stroke of genius. *The Sydney Morning Herald* reported on 4 September 2001 that a 'whopping 77 per cent of Australians support John Howard's decision to refuse the Tampa asylum seekers entry to Australia and 74 per cent approve of his handling of the subsequent crisis'. This of course does not detract from the proposition that the Howard Government was prepared to draft, and subsequently enacted, legislation that amounted to codified tyranny. And for what purpose? Electoral advantage. Fundamental liberal values were ruthlessly dispatched to the boundary and beyond. And it worked politically.

While the Border Protection Bill did not pass the Senate, it certainly meant that legislators and ministers would be far more cavalier with the rule of law and protection of fundamental rights in the future. Shortly after the Tampa incident, Ruddock opened fire on the rights of asylum seekers. Once again liberal values, particularly the rule of law, had come under attack. Ruddock's new legislation curtailed the right of asylum seekers to access the court; islands off the Australian coast, such as Christmas Island, were declared not to be part of Australia; offshore detention regimes on Nauru and Manus Island were established and the definition of 'refugee' was tightened.

The manipulation by Howard, Ruddock and Minister for Defence Peter Reith of images of asylum seekers holding their small children on a leaky boat was a demonstrably clear example of the tactic still used today with depressing regularity by governments – both those that are allegedly liberal and those that are illiberal. Fake news undermines the right to freedom of speech and the importance of an independent media.

Much has been written about the Children Overboard affair but it is worth recounting the essential elements and subsequent revelations so that one can, now with the benefit of hindsight, see that it was nothing more and nothing less than an exercise in peddling fake news for political gain and in the process further demonise a group of people that the Howard Government had effectively cast as a threat to Australia.

It reminded one of the unerringly accurate observation of the German philosopher Hannah Arendt in her seminal work *Between Past and Future*, originally published in 1961:

> The result of a consistent and total substitution of lies for factual truth is not that the lie will now be accepted as truth and truth be defamed as a lie, but that the sense by which we take our bearings in the real world – and the category of truth versus falsehood is among the mental means to this end – is being destroyed.[7]

In the early days of the 2001 election campaign, Minister for Immigration and Multicultural Affairs Philip Ruddock announced that a Navy ship, HMAS *Adelaide*, had intercepted a boat carrying asylum seekers. The boat, given the Orwellian name 'SIEV-4' (Suspected Illegal Entry Vehicle 4), was being towed out of Australian waters and Ruddock said there were reports of the passengers on the boat trying to throw their children overboard. Ruddock said that this was one of the most disturbing practices he had come across. The storyline pitched by Ruddock fed neatly into Howard's anti–asylum seeker pitch. 'I don't want people like that in Australia,' he infamously said.

Three days after Ruddock's 7 October announcement, Peter Reith released photographs of asylum seekers in the water. The problem was that the photographs did not show children being thrown into the water and it was taken a day after the supposed events took place.

A Senate Committee reported on the events in 2002 after hearing evidence from a range of witnesses. Here is a summary of what it found in relation to the 'news' and reportage angle of the issue:

> A report that a child or children had been thrown overboard from SIEV 4 arose from a telephone conversation between senior Navy officers on 7 October 2001 and the Howard government was advised of that report.
>
> Photographs released to the media on 10 October as evidence of children thrown overboard on 7 October were actually pictures taken the following day, 8 October, while SIEV 4 was sinking.
>
> By 11 October 2001, the naval chain of command had concluded that no children had been thrown overboard from SIEV 4. The Chief of Defence Force, Admiral Chris Barrie, was informed at the very least that there were serious doubts attaching to the report.
>
> On 11 October 2001, Minister Reith and his staff were separately informed that the photographs were not of the alleged children overboard events of 7 October, but were of the foundering of SIEV 4 on 8 October.
>
> On or about 17 October 2001, Admiral Barrie informed Minister Reith that there were serious doubts about the veracity of the report that children had been thrown overboard from SIEV 4.
>
> On 7 November 2001, the then Acting Chief of Defence Force, Air Marshal Angus Houston, informed Minister Reith that children had not been thrown overboard from SIEV 4.
>
> On four other occasions the lack of or dubious nature of evidence for the 'children overboard' report were drawn

to the attention of the Minister or his staff by officers from Defence.

On no occasion did the Defence organisation produce any evidence to the [Prime Minister's department and the Prime Minister's office] and which corroborated the original report that children had been thrown overboard. However no definitive advice was provided that it did not occur.

On 7 November 2001, Minister Reith informed the Prime Minister that, at the least, there were doubts about whether the photographs represented the alleged children overboard incident or whether they represented events connected with SIEV 4's sinking.

Despite direct media questioning on the issue, no correction, retraction or communication about the existence of doubts in connection with either the alleged incident itself or the photographs as evidence for it was made by any member of the Federal Government before the election on 10 November 2001.[8]

The bottom line on the Children Overboard affair was neatly described by journalist Virginia Trioli in *The Sydney Morning Herald* on 1 September 2012:

As defence minister, Reith, as well as John Howard and Philip Ruddock, promulgated the great untruth that asylum seekers had thrown their children in the water. And despite his office learning within hours of his statement that this was untrue, Reith did not correct the record at that time and did not admit he had been told his statement was false.

While this was not the first time, by any stretch of the imagination, that politicians and political parties had distorted, lied and misled – think, for example, of the appalling propaganda peddled by the political class in Australia about the Vietnam War – this was a case of the deception being blatant and *intentionally* peddled in order to maintain a political advantage.

The damage to liberal values from fake news is not only, as noted earlier, that it undermines the right of voters to make informed choices during an election campaign based on facts, and that it undermines the notion of freedom of speech and freedom of the press, but also that it disrespects humanity. The victims of the Children Overboard affair were the men, women and children on SIEV-4. They were dehumanised and used as political cannon fodder by a cynical group of politicians. Their human rights were completely disregarded.

9/11 and the 'war on terror'

Less than a month before the Children Overboard scandal broke, the world had reeled at the terrible events of 11 September 2001, the day terrorism came to the United States of America on an unprecedented and devastating scale. The attacks on the Twin Towers and the Pentagon, the loss of life and the eventual toll taken on the entire Western world was, as we know, life changing.

The events of 9/11 saw the rise of some of the most illiberal legislation ever to hit the statute books of not only the USA – with its (again, Orwellian termed) Patriot Act – but also Australia, with a raft of legislation passed in 2002 and 2003 by the Howard Government, supported by the ALP.

In terms of the adverse impact on liberal values such as the open society, the rule of law, freedom of speech and freedom of association, the significance of the anti-terror laws regime should not be underestimated. One of the leading constitutional scholars in Australia today, George Williams, noted that, while there were 'many prior examples of the federal Parliament enacting national security legislation that conferred broad powers on government agencies and had a significant impact upon individual liberty', those laws were passed in the finite context of world wars I and II. And, Professor Williams observed, those 'wartime legal measures ceased to operate after the conflict ended'. But there is no end point for the post 9/11 anti-terror laws regime. Those laws have taken on, Professor Williams writes, 'a character of permanence. Indeed, what has been called the "war on terror" has run now for a longer period than either of those worldwide conflicts, and continues unabated with no likely end in sight'.[9]

There are over seventy anti-terror laws on Australia's statute books today. Professor Williams and his colleagues calculated that, from 11 September 2001 to the fall of the Howard Liberal–National coalition government at the federal election held on 24 November 2007, the federal parliament enacted forty-eight of these laws, an average of 7.7 pieces of legislation each year:

> On average, a new anti-terror statute was passed every 6.7 weeks during the post-9/11 life of the Howard Government. In the main, these laws attracted bipartisan agreement and were enacted with the support of the Labor opposition.[10]

The illiberal nature of the laws is manifold. These are laws that define terrorism so broadly that a person can end up in jail for two or three decades even if they had no specific terror target or even a means of carrying out a terrorist attack; that make it an offence punishable by imprisonment to download material from the Internet; that make it an offence to talk about terrorist acts even without doing anything more; that provide for secret evidence to be used against an accused person yet not shared with the accused; that allow for ASIO and police to interview a person who is incommunicado; that allow for controls to be imposed on where a person can travel, who they can associate with, and where they can live … all without any need for that person to have been found guilty of an offence. This is by no means a complete list of the ways in which liberal values are undermined by Australia's anti-terror laws passed in the first years after 9/11.

The unquestioning and unwavering commitment by the Howard Government and the ALP to stand shoulder to shoulder with the USA after 9/11 meant that the 'war on terror' (as the response was termed by President George W Bush) came to Australia whether there was a real threat or not. During times of 'war', says Jeffrey C Isaac, Professor of Political Science at Indiana University, 'liberal values are placed under duress' and

> There are at least two mutually reinforcing sources of this pressure … One is the preoccupation with national security and the tendency of political leaders and state agencies to monitor society and police its borders, both geographic

> and mental, under the guise of this concern. The second is the fear of designated enemies, and of vulnerability in general, that war inevitably engenders in civilian populations.[11]

This held true in Australia after 9/11, as it did in the USA and other Western nations such as the United Kingdom. In other words, the power and paternalism vested in the Australian body politic was used to a maximum extent, and dissenting liberal values arguments were simply cast aside because of the pressures described by Professor Isaac.

The legacies

Pauline Hanson's unbridled right-wing populism, the Tampa incident and the subsequent Children Overboard affair, together with the manic legislative activity of the post 9/11 environment, are not merely of historical interest; they were key milestones in the decline of liberal values in this nation. And their legacy is with us still. They each represent a shift in how political parties, governments and the community have dealt with challenges to liberal values.

Hanson is still with us, and her toxic populism resonates with some marginal-seat voters in her home state of Queensland. The already-well-to-the-right-of-centre Liberals and Nationals, pushed by fear of Hanson in that state, dumped Prime Minister Malcolm Turnbull because, despite his having jettisoned much of his liberal outlook in order to hold his government together, was perceived as still being too liberal. The failure of one prime minister in 1996 to stand up to Hanson and what she stood for gave intolerance, racism, and the politics of resentment an opportunity to flourish as it does today. As to Howard's argument that any criticism of her would have made her more popular, this is not the point. Because Howard was never committed to liberal values, and because he used the politics of resentment to court his so-called 'battlers', giving Hanson leeway was a matter of pure convenience.

And the legacy of Tampa? The Tampa incident notoriously set off the cruel and internationally condemned offshore detention regime and the politics of border security. While it is true that mandatory detention began in the dying days of the Keating Government, the fact is that the harshness of the regime was a notable characteristic of the post-Tampa hysteria whipped up jointly by a politically insecure prime minister facing a difficult election and his loyal foot soldier Philip Ruddock.

The Tampa incident stripped the humanity and individuality of those seeking asylum in Australia. It made it much easier for the Australian community and politicians across the spectrum – with only a few notable exceptions, such as the Australian Democrats, the Greens, a handful of Liberal backbenchers and now cross-benchers like Andrew Wilkie from Tasmania – to obsess over 'stopping the boats' and do so by illiberal policies such as detaining individuals and their children for lengthy periods with grossly inadequate health care.

The commitment of Australia to compliance with international liberal values, expressed through treaties and conventions on human rights and refugees, has been cast aside by both major political parties in this country. They have shamelessly pursued an awful neocolonialism towards impoverished and hopelessly corrupt nations like Papua New Guinea and Nauru.

So embedded is the post-Tampa world of faceless asylum seekers that the media, again with notable exceptions, rarely report on the mountains of evidence about the deliberate infliction by the Australian Government of calculated cruelty designed to make those in detention give up hope and head back to persecution, famine and war. Worse still, the Tampa crisis ushered in an era of extraordinary arrogance that dismisses any criticism of the detention of asylum seekers. Critics are either ignored or hounded. The former president of the Australian Human Rights Commission, Gillian Triggs, was bullied and undermined by the Abbott Government and its allies in the media, mainly News Limited. Her 'sin'? Writing a scathing report about the intolerable conditions in immigration detention for asylum seekers. Former prime minister Tony Abbott angrily dismissed one of the many United Nations reports that has criticised and condemned the detention policy. According to Abbott, Australians are sick and tired of being lectured to by the UN. This is the sort of rhetoric that authoritarian leaders use when stung by reality from the UN.

As *The Age* noted in an editorial of 28 January 2016:

> Australians prefer to believe they look out for the most disadvantaged members of our community. But there is an increasing disconnection between the high standards the nation professes to pursue and the contemptuous policies implemented by governments that have the effect

of eroding human rights or denying our obligations under international law.

That disconnection was spawned from the contemptuous treatment of all associated with the *Tampa* in 2001.

And the Children Overboard affair ensured that the narrative about asylum seekers would forever be about presentation of a danger: the inhuman hordes on their leaky boats are threatening the borders of this vast continent – they must be stopped; they represent an existential threat to the Australian way of life … So potent is the demonising of the asylum seeker that even the ALP refuses to consider an end to the institutional cruelty of offshore detention, despite internal pressure from those with a belief that liberal values should be practised as well as preached.

Along with Tampa, the Children Overboard scandal turned the natural and inevitable movement of people to free themselves from life-threatening circumstances and seek a safe and secure life into a war waged by Australia. And, like the 'war on terror', this would be a never-ending war. It also encouraged the culture of secrecy that now surrounds the movement of boats carrying asylum seekers. Operation Sovereign Borders, a policy devised by Scott Morrison and announced during the 2013 federal election, would ensure there was no repeat of politicians being exposed as misleading the people and lying about boats or of revelations about how politicians created serious conflicts for military commanders. Operation Sovereign Borders was, and still is, a top-secret military operation in respect of which there would be no scrutiny by anyone – literally.

Sociologist Ben Wadham, writing in *The Conversation* on 8 January 2014, asked:

> Can we be confident that our commanders are not subject to inappropriate policy advice from Canberra? Are they subject to duress from the potential of political reprisal for placing their maritime obligations above the obligations of their political masters? The current reporting arrangements mean that Operation Sovereign Borders is unable to be effectively questioned.

But what Children Overboard also did was make it perfectly acceptable for politicians and the media to practise the dark art of 'fake news'. The reality is that, despite the uncovering of deception on the part of the Howard Government, the government got away with it.

The legacy of 9/11 and the 'war on terror' rolls on. To quote George Williams again, this time writing in 2016:

> Since September 2001, enacting laws or regulations that infringe democratic freedoms has become a routine part of the legislative process. Basic values such as freedom of speech are not only being impugned in the name of national security or counter-terrorism, but for a range of mundane purposes. Speech offences now apply to a range of public places and occupations, and legislatures have greatly expanded the capacity of state agencies to detain people without charge or arrest. Such offences have become so normal and accepted that they can be turned into law without eliciting a community or media response.

Whether it's members of bikie gangs, environmental protestors, trade unionists or ordinary citizens accused of a crime, it is now de rigueur to shred liberal values because legislators – supported by a lazy, or in some cases highly supportive, media (except of course when it comes to protecting themselves and their interests, in which case they become alarmed by the decline of liberal values) – get away with it.

The past two decades have been deeply depressing for those in the community who think liberal values are the stuff of democratic societies. In fact, with the exception of some human rights laws passed in Victoria and the ACT over the past decade, no legislation has been passed in Australia that has either restored a lost human right or enhanced human rights. And since the end of the reign of Gillian Triggs at the Human Rights Commission (the one watchdog on the decline of liberal values), any word from that organisation has been, shall we say, *sotto voce*.

CHAPTER 3

The Tools of Populism: Elites, Ordinary Australians, 'The Other'

The populist right prides itself on being the voice of 'ordinary Australians'. Former prime minister John Howard used to talk about 'ordinary' or 'mainstream' Australians and 'battlers'. In fact, so potent was Howard's technique that a fellow conservative, Canadian Prime Minister Stephen Harper, who in 2015 lost office to the most liberal of leaders, Justin Trudeau, started peppering his speech with the phrase 'ordinary Canadians'.

Populists from the right everywhere claim that they speak for 'ordinary' people and that they are opposed to the 'elites'. Whether it be Hungarian Prime Minister Viktor Orbán; Nigel Farage, who spearheaded the Brexit campaign; or Pauline Hanson in Australia, all use the term 'elites' with contempt and wrap themselves in the cloak of ordinariness.

Language is very important to populists, as is their identification with a world view scorning a university-educated globalist elite that has for too long dictated what 'ordinary' people should think and how they should act. The favoured line of argument for the populist right is to state with conviction that it is 'political correctness' that is stifling the views of 'ordinary' people. The 'elites', of course, police 'political correctness'.

Linked to these notions is extreme fear of 'The Other'. As we noted in the previous chapter, whipping up fear of 'The Other' is powerful and is designed to play on the vulnerability and insecurity of communities and the individuals within them who feel exposed by social and economic change. 'The Other' is the migrant, the Indigenous, the Muslim and, in many quarters, the transgender person (according to Prime Minister Scott Morrison there are 'transgender whisperers' in our schools). As described by political scientist Richard Pithouse of the University of the Witwatersrand:

> Today the right is on the rise across much of Europe, including Italy, Austria and Germany, and Sweden. The new right is explicitly constituted around hostility to the migrant. The same politics festers in Europe's settler colonies, particularly in Australia and the United States.[1]

That the populist right use common language and themes is evident by even a cursory examination of the utterances of the likes of Orbán, Farage and, in Australia, Howard and his acolytes such as Dutton and Morrison.

Orbán, in a speech delivered in 2018, said that in 'today's open-society Europe there are no borders; European people can be readily replaced with immigrants; the family has been transformed into an optional, fluid form of cohabitation; the nation, national identity and national pride are seen as negative and obsolete notions; and the state no longer guarantees security in Europe.'[2]

Nigel Farage tweeted, after speaking on Sky News Australia on 2 September 2018: 'There's been a great crisis of conservatism and a huge disconnect between the ruling elites and ordinary people, made worse by career politics.'

In the Australian context, John Howard, addressing the Liberal Party faithful on March 15 1998, said he was leading a party

> that was owned by no one section of the Australian community … a party for all Australians. It wasn't owned by the business community. It wasn't owned by the noisy elites. It wasn't owned by political correctness. It certainly wasn't owned by the trade union movement. It was owned by the ordinary men and women of Australia.

On his elevation to prime minister status in 2018, Morrison zeroed in on 'ordinary Australians'. 'We [the Liberal Government] are on your side,' he said, 'because we share beliefs and values in common, as you go about everything you do each day.'

According to Dutton, when Paul Keating was Australian prime minister people were walking around 'on eggshells' because of political correctness; the ALP leader Bill Shorten is 'part of the tricky elite in this country'; and lawyers who act for asylum seekers on a pro bono basis are part of the problem of 'political correctness' and are 'un-Australian'.

Populist-right politicians work hand in glove with their allies in the media. On 22 July 2018, former foreign minister and

Australian high commissioner to London, Alexander Downer, penned an opinion piece for the *Financial Review* that dripped with loathing about a visit he had made to 'a well-known magazine' in London. In a thinly veiled reference to journalists at *The Guardian*, he said:

> They – and their magazine – are spear throwers for liberal internationalism. They rejoice in the practice of salami-slicing society with identity politics, affirmative action for everyone except white males, they abhor restrictions on immigration, they think new technologies will create mass unemployment and they are sure the rise of Trump, Brexit and what they call 'populist' parties is caused by large swathes of Western society 'missing out'.

Why he didn't mention the name of the journal who invited him in was mystifying.

The media preferred by Dutton and Downer include presenters on Sky News who also have columns in newspapers such as the *Herald Sun*, *The Daily Telegraph* and *The Australian*. Andrew Bolt, Paul Murray, Peta Credlin and Chris Kenny, along with the self-styled 'outsiders' Rowan Dean and Ross Cameron (replaced now by veteran right-wing populist Piers Akerman), bat for populism, wage war on 'political correctness' and the 'elites', and purport to represent and speak for 'ordinary Australians'. These warriors are, of course, relative newcomers in terms of the populist cause. Sydney broadcasters Alan Jones and Ray Hadley have been running the right-wing populist agenda for decades. But what all of those mentioned here do share is a modus operandi of unbridled aggression against what they describe as 'the left'.

The populist right's tool kit

The tool kit of the right-wing populist is a very powerful one. Included in it are terms such as 'elites' and 'political correctness', which they have successfully appropriated. Let's start with the notion of 'political correctness'.

Two weeks before Christmas 2016, the Immigration minister, Peter Dutton, got angry. Appearing on his favourite soapbox, radio station 2GB's Ray Hadley program, Dutton heard that a constituent of his had rung the radio station to complain that, at a Brisbane primary school's end-of-year concert, the words of the carol 'We Wish You a Merry Christmas' were changed to 'We wish you a happy holiday'.

This was too much for the minister. 'You make my blood boil with these stories,' he fumed. 'It is political correctness gone mad and I think people have just had enough of it.' So what needed to happen, because people had 'had a gutful' of political correctness, Dutton told Hadley and his listeners, was that we needed 'to rise up against it'. 'People need to speak against it as they are [doing],' he said.[3]

(It did not seem to concern Dutton or Hadley that the school in fact was revelling in traditional Christmas activities. A quick glance at the Kedron State School's website reveals there is no shortage of Christmas cheer at the north Brisbane school. 'On December 2, the school held a P&C Christmas stall and Christmas concert, which featured carols,' the *Brisbane Times* reported on 16 December, 2016. The school's online diary also advertised the Kedron Church of Christ Christmas concert on December 4. And in his final newsletter of the year, the principal wished families a 'safe, happy Christmas' and celebrated the recently held 'magical Christmas evening', the *Brisbane Times* assured its readers.)

While Dutton was urging the populace to take up their cultural pitchforks, a conservative academic, Kevin Donnelly, was publishing a book arguing that 'political correctness' is so cancerous that it represents an existential threat to Australia. According to Donnelly, whose book *How Political Correctness Is Destroying Australia – Enemies Within and Without* was launched jointly by former prime minister Tony Abbott and radio shock jock Alan Jones in June 2018, 'the reality is that Australia is also facing an existential threat involving a virulent and powerful political correctness movement and, similar to Europe, the adverse impact of immigration and Islamic terrorism'. Promoting his book, Donnelly noted in an article for *The Spectator* that, 'while examples like Qantas asking its flight attendants to stop using "mum" and "dad", Sydney University's debating club enforcing gender diversity and Israel Folau being attacked as homophobic for criticising gays are recent examples, the political correctness movement has been active for years.'[4] According to Donnelly and those who share this apocalyptic view, it's a case of 'reds under beds' dusted off and rebranded. 'Political correctness' from this perspective is a form of cultural Marxism that is intent on pursuing class war and delivering the end of the capitalist Christian society.

The crusader against 'political correctness' and cultural Marxism sees him- or herself as the upholder of the liberal values of freedom of speech and thought. It is the 'politically correct' brigade, we are told, whose members are found naturally in universities, the public service, the ABC and the arts, who are the enemies of liberal values. Writing in *The Australian* on 31 August 2018, Stephen Chavura, a teacher at a Catholic college in Sydney, argued that those who prosecute the cause of political correctness 'can never embrace freedom of speech, because it ultimately seeks to shape and control culture, which cannot be shaped and controlled so long as one of the greatest shapers of culture – speech – is beyond its control'. According to Chavura, a form of cultural terror is being waged against dissenters:

> Doctors who question transgender ideology will be harassed, activists and intellectuals who question multiculturalism will be demonised, conservative intellectuals will be no-platformed, all with the co-operation of the police, universities, and human rights and anti-discrimination commissions.[5]

In reality, the positioning of the critics of 'political correctness' as being suborned – or having to walk 'on eggshells', to use Dutton's phrase – is not only absurd but breathtakingly hypocritical.

As to the latter, one only has to reflect on two individuals who dared to comment critically about Anzac Day, a national memorial day which has, since the Howard era, become little more than an exercise in uncritical nationalism. A former SBS journalist, Scott McIntyre, and a young woman who had appeared on ABC TV, Yassmin Abdel-Magied, were subjected to the blowtorch of the populist right for daring to exercise the right of freedom of speech and thought on this subject.

The cases of Abdel-Magied and McIntyre illustrate not only the hypocrisy of the populist right when it comes to its assertion that it is the true champion of freedom of speech and thoughts, but the fact that it is vicious in how it deals with its 'enemies'.

Scott McIntyre was a sports journalist at SBS when, on Anzac Day 2015, he tweeted that some of those celebrating or remembering the day were 'poorly read, largely white, nationalist drinkers and gamblers'. He also wrote: 'Remembering the summary execution, widespread rape and theft committed by these "brave" Anzacs in Egypt, Palestine and Japan', and 'Not forgetting that the largest single-day terrorist attacks in history were committed by this nation & their allies in Hiroshima & Nagasaki'.

The more or less liberal Malcolm Turnbull used his official Twitter account to condemn McIntyre, who was subsequently sacked from SBS for refusing, said the broadcaster, to comply with its guidelines.

The lions of the populist right lined up on cue to attack McIntyre. Andrew Bolt wrote in the *Herald Sun*: 'Of all "hate speech" now, McIntyre's is becoming the most dangerous. He had to go.' Bolt's Sydney counterpart, Miranda Devine, used words such as 'obnoxious' and 'loathsome' and sneeringly commented that McIntyre 'continues to be free to tweet whatever garbage he likes and will probably be rewarded with a job at the Guardian – or maybe a column at Fairfax', she wrote in *The Daily Telegraph* on 29 April, 2015. To be fair, she didn't think it was a sackable offence.

Meanwhile, Chris Kenny, writing in the Adelaide *Advertiser*, saw through the lens of 'elites' versus 'mainstream Australians' all those who supported McIntyre. 'This is the progressive media, academic and political class that likes to think it is intellectually and morally superior to the rest of the nation,' opined Kenny. 'But this episode has shown, yet again, that if you want good sense, strong judgment and fair values you are more likely to find them in the Australian mainstream.' A *Daily Telegraph* columnist, Justin Smith, said that McIntyre was a 'halfwit'.

But the personal abuse aimed at McIntyre and claims of his being part of some public broadcaster 'elites' versus the 'ordinary Australians' was nothing compared with the extraordinary and depressingly nasty savaging by the populist right on Abdel-Magied.

On Anzac Day 2017, Abdel-Magied posted on her Facebook page the message 'LEST. WE. FORGET. (Manus, Nauru, Syria, Palestine...).' She then removed it and later apologised (one wonders why, given that her point about death and war was a valid one). Not only did the ABC remove her as host of its program *Australia Wide*, but Abdel-Magied was abused, vilified, threatened and harassed by the populist right. Her life in Australia became hell – so much so, she moved to the United Kingdom.

The Daily Telegraph ran a front page that ran like this: 'ABC host's ultimate insult to Anzac legend. Two Finger Salute. Un-Australian broadcaster backs activist who demeans our war heroes.' Leaving aside the curious proposition that Anzac is a legend, this headline could have been dreamed up in the editorial office of any dictatorship-run news outlet anywhere.

A few months later, in a piece on Abdel-Magied in August 2017, investigative journalist Melissa Fyfe summarised the abuse endured by this young engineering graduate.

> She was accused of a 'vile slur' against dead Australian soldiers, of using a sacred day to make a political point about refugees. Death threats started arriving. Videos of beheadings and rapes clogged her email and Twitter account. She had to move house and change her phone number. Senior politicians called for her to be deported and sacked from a part-time ABC TV gig. Outraged Sky News host Paul Murray struggled to get his mouth around 'this sheila's' name. 'I've mispronounced,' he said. 'But who cares?'[6]

One of the populist right's complaints about Abdel-Magied was that the ABC should not have someone like her on its books. The then deputy prime minister, Barnaby Joyce, appeared to take the view that the ABC would lose funding because of this fact.

'They make life exceedingly difficult for people like myself on the expenditure review committee when we're fighting for funds,' Joyce said, 'when issues such as this are brought up to us.' Channelling the notoriously illiberal remarks of his colleague and now fellow backbencher, Tony Abbott, who once complained that the ABC appeared to be on everyone's side except Australia's, Joyce lamented:

> It starts to become a sense that the culture of the ABC in some instances is at odds with the culture of Australia …

you can't just have one of your paid presenters making a statement like that.

When the ABC buckled and failed to uphold the liberal values of freedom of speech and freedom of expression by cancelling Abdel-Magied's program a month after Anzac Day, Peter Dutton told Ray Hadley's 2GB program 'One down, many to go.'

That Abdel-Magied is a woman, not an Anglo-European but Muslim, and with names that reflect her Sudanese heritage, meant that the level of disrespect shown her was greater than that shown McIntyre. The comment from Sky News's Paul Murray, noted above – 'this sheila's name … I've mispronounced, but who cares?' – was just one example.

While the populist right, or at least some of their number, paraded their 'commitment' to freedom of speech and expression and contrasted themselves as being 'better than the Left who silence dissenting voices', to quote the *Herald Sun* columnist Rita Panahi on 27 April 2017, the reality is that they are intolerant of freedom of thought and word. It is a case of the populist right being, to paraphrase Shakespeare, hoist with its own petard.

Ironically, the hypocrisy of the cry from the populist right about 'political correctness', that the left is censorious and intolerant of alternative views and speech, and that, to return to the mythology perpetuated by Howard and more latterly Dutton, people were walking around on 'eggshells' because of the plague of political correctness that was allegedly evident in the Keating government era, is no better illustrated than by the way in which the populist right dealt with the McIntyre and Abdel-Magied matters.

In both cases Anzac Day was deemed to be so sacred, so holy, that it amounts to a form of blasphemy for any person to deviate from the script. A script which, by the way, was manipulated by Howard and the populist right to push a crude brand of Australian nationalism – or, to quote a neat phrase used by political scientist Aurelien Mondon, an 'ethno-exclusivist vision of Australian nationalism'.

Refusing to allow a contest of views, ideas and expressions about Anzac Day and what it stands for or reminds us about, other than a barracking for Australian soldiers dead and alive, is extraordinary censorship. In fact, so visceral is the hatred and contempt for the actions of McIntyre and Abdel-Magied that personal abuse, threats to organisations associated with them, and effectively telling them to zip it is deemed appropriate by the populist right.

The pall of political correctness is of course an invention of the populist right to bully, demean and therefore silence its critics.

What is extraordinary is the lack of introspection on the part of the populist right. Commentators like Devine and Panahi no doubt believe they are committed to the liberal values of freedom of speech and thought – or at least let us not assume that they are anything but genuine in that belief – but their conduct in both McIntyre's and Abdel-Magied's cases says that they are not. While they write that McIntyre and Abdel-Magied should not have been sacked, their intolerance of what was said by both, exemplified by the abusive and derisory contempt in their language, tells us otherwise.

Another populist-right commentator, Tim Blair, called the treatment of Abdel-Magied a rebuke. On 27 April 2017, Blair wrote: 'Criticism is an integral part of freedom of speech. Abdel-Magied is free to speak her mind. Critics are free to rebuke her.' Apparently his nasty personal attack on Abdel-Magied, calling her a 'wayward ABC staffer', is what he means by rebuke. To rebuke an individual is to criticise what they said, and perhaps to say the words ought not to have been said or they were insensitive. But Blair's *Daily Telegraph* colleagues who put together the extraordinary headline were doing far more than simply rebuking Abdel-Magied.

It is also the case that the rabid response to what McIntyre and Abdel-Magied said can, as explicitly recognised by the quote from the Adelaide *Advertiser*'s Chris Kenny, be seen through the populist-right lens of 'elites' against 'ordinary Australians'. The profiling of Scott McIntyre and Yassmin Abdel-Magied as media personalities taking a pay cheque from the 'left-wing' public broadcasting machine, and the latter being a Muslim woman, is relevant here given the subject matter.

Case Mudde, a political scientist at the University of Georgia in the United States of America, notes that the populist right sees a 'distinction between the elite and the people' that is 'not based on how much money you have or even what kind of position you have. It's based on your values'. Professor Mudde's point is highlighted by Kenny's remark that 'good sense, strong judgment and fair values' are 'more likely to [be found] in the Australian mainstream' than among 'the progressive media, academic and political class'. In short, moral superiority is deemed to lie with the 'ordinary' people.

'The Other'

The treatment of Yassmin Abdel-Magied by the populist right was a demonstration of the phenomenon of 'The Other'. One of the most potent and illiberal tools of the right is the way in which it portrays groups such as Indigenous Australians, asylum seekers and Muslims as being somehow less than human or – in some cases, such as via the medium of imagery – in a stereotypical way.

We saw it in the Tampa and Children Overboard sagas. The language and actions of politicians in both cases were constructed around the narrative that there is 'us' and there is 'them'. Pauline Hanson's attack on foreign aid and Indigenous welfare fits within the same narrative.

There is nothing new in this narrative. The late Palestinian-born scholar Edward Saïd developed the concept of 'The Other' in his seminal work *Orientalism*, first published in 1978. The concept of seeing some of humanity in terms of 'The Other' means 'disregarding, essentialising, denuding the humanity of another culture, people or geographical region'. And once that is done, as renowned author and activist Naomi Klein remarked in 2016,

> the ground is softened for any transgression: violent expulsion, land theft, occupation, invasion. Because the whole point of othering is that the other doesn't have the same rights, the same humanity, as those making the distinction.[7]

It becomes unpatriotic to support and advocate for 'The Other'. This is why Peter Dutton can term lawyers who act for asylum seekers as 'un-Australian'. It explains former prime minister Tony Abbott's claim on Ray Hadley's 2GB program of 4 February 2014 that 'it dismays Australians when the national broadcaster appears to take everyone's side but its own and I think it is a problem'. He was referring to reporting by the ABC of the Edward Snowden leaks and the claims of abuse of asylum seekers.

Dutton's use of the narrative of 'The Other' was noticeable in his remarks made in an interview with *The Daily Telegraph*'s Miranda Devine in March 2018 about white South African farmers. Responding to reports of the predominantly black South African parliament looking at expropriation of white farmers' land without compensation, Dutton said, 'If you look at the footage and read the stories, you hear the accounts, it's a horrific circumstance they face.' He went on to say these farmers 'need help from a civilised country like ours'. And why help South African farmers?

> We want people who want to come here, abide by our laws, integrate into our society, work hard, not lead a life on welfare. And I think these people deserve special attention and we're certainly applying that special attention now.

In other words, post-apartheid South Africa is not 'civilised' like Anglo-European Australia and because white farmers are 'us' then they will not be like asylum seekers from Iraq, Afghanistan, Iran and Sri Lanka when it comes to 'fitting in' and working hard.

And the 'Other-ness' of the continent of Africa is utilised by Dutton and other conservatives to whip up fear in Melbourne. On 3 January 2018, Dutton, again being interviewed on 2GB (one gets the picture), observed that because of 'African gangs' who were alleged to have committed crimes, Victorians are 'scared to go out to restaurants'. And what is more, Victorians are amazed by 'the jokes of sentences being handed down' which is caused, of course, by the 'political correctness that's taken hold'. A day before Dutton's interview, Health Minister Greg Hunt, who some describe as apparently more liberal than conservative, claimed that African gang crime is 'out of control'. Seven months later, on 17 July 2018, then prime minister Malcolm Turnbull weighed in to fuel the fire.

In Dutton's interview we have the weaving of two potent attack tools of the populist right in one interview. There is no logic or rationality in these remarks, but that is not the point. The idea is that 'The Other' is to be guarded against because it is dangerous. And the 'elite' judges and magistrates do not have the 'ordinary' Victorian's interests at heart because they are too busy being 'politically correct'.

In fact, according to Rita Panahi of the *Herald Sun*, the presence of gangs of young people who commit crimes is the fault of the 'left' and 'political correctness'. 'The ideologues of the left who want to blame poverty, isolation and racism for the rise of ethnic gangs are part of the problem. In their eagerness to blame societal ills, real and imagined, they absolve these violent thugs of any responsibility,' fumed Panahi in a column published on 26 April 2016.

That crime and antisocial activity are part and parcel of 'Other-ness' is a standard line from the populist right. The *Herald Sun*'s Andrew Bolt took to feverishly reporting allegations of criminal activity where descriptions of persons being of 'African appearance' was used. His point was to show that those who argued that the idea of 'African gangs' was a myth were wrong. It did not seem to occur to Bolt that using the term 'crimes committed' when cataloguing these reports was plain wrong. The cases had not been through the courts, for a start. And simply because a witness says a person is of 'African appearance' does not mean that they are from one of many countries making up that vast continent.

Perhaps the most egregiously populist effort on the Victorian 'African gangs' issue has come from the tabloid *Sunday Night* program on Channel 7. On 8 July 2018 the program broadcast a piece by journalist Alex Cullen that claimed, wrongly, that Victoria Police won't talk about crime problems in some African communities because 'we live in such politically correct times'. The summary of the program on Channel 7's website claimed:

> Barely a week goes by when there's not a report in the news. African gangs running riot, terrorising, robbing, wreaking havoc. Yet we live in such politically correct times that, in Victoria, police have been loath to admit there's even a problem.

The program interviewed an understandably upset and traumatised victim of two robberies that were said to have been committed by 'armed African criminals'. The victim wanted the perpetrators deported 'back to where they came from'.

The populist right hits back against claims that it is racist to identify the ethnicity of individuals and groups allegedly involved in crime. They are doing the right thing, runs the rhetoric, by telling us the 'truth' and not being bound by 'political correctness'. On 18 August 2018 another of the Sky News stable, Paul Murray, argued self-pityingly in a *Gold Coast Bulletin* column that by stating there has been an 'obvious uptick in attacks by gangs of teenagers with clear family roots back to Africa', he will be viewed 'as one of the evil souls' by those in Victoria who were disturbed by the racist undertones of the rhetoric surrounding the so-called 'African gangs' issue.

The approach of Murray and those who have been banging the 'Victorian African gangs crime wave' drum is intellectually disingenuous. The number of column inches, airplay minutes and comments from federal politicians like Dutton on what is a state political and policy matter can only be explained by its being underpinned by the narrative of 'The Other'.

Consider this. Have we seen the populist-right commentariat and politicians obsessing over crimes allegedly committed by Anglo-Europeans? Do we see reference in columns by Bolt to 'persons of English appearance'? The answer to both questions is no. Yet there are, and always have been, numerous alliances of Anglo-European individuals, called gangs, that break the law.

A key reason for the populist right's pursuit of the 'Victorian African gangs' issue has been because it assists their political allies in the conservative parties to blame the Labor government of Victorian Premier Daniel Andrews. More important, though, is the reason that it feeds into a populist desire to divide society into those who belong and those who do not. It is, as we noted above, a standard tactic of the populist right to demonise those who are not perceived to be 'ordinary Australians'. As John Budarick, a lecturer in Media at Adelaide University, has observed:

> Not only do racial labels implicate all Africans in violent crime, they also keep alive that most pernicious of links between race and behaviour. If the race of offenders is the only part of their identity worth mentioning in news reports, then it stands to reason this has a causal link with their behaviour. Other complex factors that contribute to crime get ignored.[8]

It fits the populist-right narrative to highlight the skin colour, nationality, religion and ethnicity of persons who are alleged to be engaged in criminal activity if that skin colour is not white, nationality not Anglo-European, religion not Christian or Jewish and ethnicity not Caucasian. It fits within a world view that seeks to identify and coalesce with the traditional community against the newcomers, the 'outsiders' seeking a place at the table. This is the language and politics of exclusion at work.

And nowhere is it more evident than in the way the populist right has dehumanised the men, women and children who embarked on dangerous boat journeys seeking asylum in the rich island continent of Australia.

So much has been written and said about the mistreatment of asylum seekers by all Australian governments over the past two decades, but particularly since the Tampa incident in 2001, that we need not traverse that territory here. Suffice to say there is an unambiguous view across institutions responsible for the promulgation, interpretation and enforcement (such as it is) of human rights and international law – whether it be at the United Nations or in well-regarded NGOs such as Human Rights Watch and Amnesty International – that the policy of indefinite detention of men, women and children in immigration detention within Australia or in horrific conditions on Manus Island and Nauru is unlawful. It is unconscionable and it has lowered the reputation of Australia globally.

The suffering endured by those in detention is equally well documented and known. The physical and mental harm, the suicides, the deaths, the breaking up of families, the deliberate placing of obstacles in the way of desperately ill detainees to receive proper health care have reached the point where, as one Canberra-based journalist said to this author, the media does not report it any longer. With the notable exceptions of outlets such as *The Guardian*, the ABC, SBS and online sites like Crikey and New Matilda, this is sadly the case.

The deliberate strategy of refusing journalists access to detention centres, particularly in the case of Nauru, does not concern too many in this country. Laws making it a criminal offence to speak about what goes on in detention centres were supported by nearly all federal MPs, with only a few decent and liberal members opposing it.

The language used to describe asylum seekers and their advocates again fits within the narrative of 'The Other'. They represent a threat to the core of right-wing populism – sovereignty and borders.

A research project published in 2013 by academics from the University of Queensland – Roland Bleiker, David Campbell, Emma Hutchison and Xzarina Nicholson – analysed media images of asylum seekers in 2001 and 2011. The authors found that *The Australian* and *The Sydney Morning Herald* 'visually portray asylum seekers in very particular, highly political and highly dehumanising ways'. The researchers also found that the 'category of image that is most likely to create compassion and empathy in viewers – photographs of individual refugees with clearly recognisable facial features – made up a remarkably low 2 per cent of all images', while 'Almost half of all images displayed no visual features at all'. The paper concluded: 'The arrival of asylum seekers is visually framed not as a humanitarian crisis that involves grievable lives requiring compassion, but primarily as a threat to Australia's sovereignty and security.'[9]

The extent to which asylum seekers have been dehumanised in the eyes of the Australian community, and particularly in the media, was borne out by virtue of the fact that Immigration Minister Peter Dutton drew little criticism for his extraordinary statement on 23 June 2018 that 'it's essential that people realise that the hard-won success of the last few years could be undone overnight by a single act of compassion in bringing 20 people from Manus to Australia.' The success to which Dutton refers is the boast of the Abbott, Turnbull and Morrison governments that they 'stopped the boats'. While the statement is a palpable lie – because all that has happened is that a veil of secrecy has been thrown over the issue by calling it a military operation – it is a potent line for right-wing populists.

In the USA it is a wall with Mexico, in Hungary a fence across that country's eastern and southern borders, and in Australia a Navy or Border Force vessel. All mean the same thing: while the 'elites' believe in open borders and are not rooted to a community, 'ordinary folk' want to feel secure and to know that their borders are safe. 'The Other' must be kept at bay at all costs, literally.

The populist right in Australia is as nativist as US President Donald Trump on the issue of border control. Like President Trump, former prime minister John Howard used the Tampa incident to project an image of a political leader who was ensuring the borders were brought under control. The media and major political parties in Australia are obsessed with border control. What happens to the individuals turned or pushed back under Operation Sovereign Borders is of no interest. Those asylum seekers on Manus Island and Nauru are to be punished for daring to enter Australian territory. They are 'illegals', apparently. Just like the 'African gangs', they are, apparently, on the wrong side of the law.

And as was the case with the savage treatment – well beyond the bounds of 'rebuke', to use Tim Blair's word – of Scott McIntyre and Yassmin Abdel-Magied by the populist right for their 'sacrilege' over Anzac Day, so it is with those in positions of influence and authority within government circles who criticise the mistreatment of asylum seekers.

The case of former president of the Australian Human Rights Commission Gillian Triggs is perhaps the worst case of bullying of an independent statutory office holder that any of us can remember. Professor Triggs's 'sin' was to open an investigation into the human rights abuses that so clearly existed, and still do exist, in immigration detention. Appointed by the Gillard Government in 2012, Professor Triggs launched an inquiry into the wellbeing of children in immigration detention in February 2014. That decision was enough to see the populist right flex its muscles and begin an extraordinary and vicious attack on Professor Triggs, which they sustained until her five-year term finished in 2017.

RMIT University's Dr Binoy Kampmark has particularised what happened to Professor Triggs. As he noted, her tenure was 'marked by verbal assault, castigation and brute cynicism from opponents in the Murdoch media, the Coalition Government and black letter lawyers. Her office has been mauled by pollster watching jackals in an establishment keen to invert the humanitarian cause.'[10] Because she had not investigated the issue of children in detention while the ALP was in office, she must be a political enemy, ran the absurd paranoid logic of the Abbott Government. And of course, once again Professor Triggs became a victim of the populist right's obsession with 'elites' and 'ordinary' Australians. According to Chris Kenny, this time writing in *The Australian* on 26 July 2017:

> [Professor Triggs's] decision to seize the limelight and become a surrogate for the great social policy battles of our time ... made her a proxy who personifies for some the nanny-state moralising and sanctimonious criticism of mainstream values by the elites, and for others the sophisticated globalism and multilateral humanitarianism that is unafraid to critique Australia's performance.

The fact that Professor Triggs's statutory duties mean she must be engaged in 'social policy battles' seemed irrelevant to Kenny.

Naturally, Professor Triggs was accused of 'political correctness' and Dutton, the ever-present warrior of the populist right, accused Professor Triggs of being a 'disgrace' and 'a political advocate' because she dared to make findings that should have shocked no one with a droplet of liberal values coursing through their veins – that children's wellbeing was at risk of serious harm by their being held in immigration detention.

The appalling bullying of Professor Triggs, who remarkably did not buckle under the assault, was the sort of illiberal episode one would find in a country like Hungary or its nativist ally Poland.

What is notable about the populist right in each of the cases discussed in this chapter is the consistent use of terms of abuse such as 'political correctness' and 'elites' and the posturing of its members as comprising the 'ordinary' Australian community. Liberal values such as openness, tolerance, freedom of speech and thought, and even civility, are jettisoned in favour of illiberal sneering and fearmongering about 'The Other' and 'elites'.

Underlying all of this is the self-justifying absurdity that the populist right is a downtrodden and persecuted group standing up for those of their number who are equally oppressed by an arrogant liberal elite. The reality, of course, is very different. With their tool kit at the ready, the populist right is on the front foot daily in the media and corridors of power, aiming fire at liberal values.

CHAPTER 4

Kill all the Judges: Decline of the Rule of Law

It was an extraordinary sight. On a winter's morning in June 2018, the nation's senior lawyer had to appear before the Chief Justice of Victoria, Marilyn Warren, and two senior colleagues. His brief was to explain why three Turnbull government ministers should not be cited for contempt of court. This was a black letter day for the rule of law in Australia.

In a liberal democracy like Australia, supposedly committed to the ideal that the judiciary and the courts they sit in are always and everywhere independent of government, the notion that politicians could be perceived as trying to influence the outcome of cases before those courts is anathema. After all, our political class and media shake their collective heads in sorrow at places such as Zimbabwe where judicial independence has been shredded by political bullying.

But, on 16 June 2018, Stephen Donaghue, the Solicitor General for the Commonwealth, found himself having to negotiate an understandably hostile bench on the one hand and the slip-sliding of his clients, Human Services Minister Alan Tudge, Health Minister Greg Hunt and Assistant Treasurer Michael Sukkar on the other. This trio, mockingly labelled the 'Yarra Three' by the opposition ALP, had provided comments to *The Australian* earlier in the week about what they thought of the sentencing practices of Victorian courts in terrorism cases, and how those compared with what occurred in New South Wales.

On 13 June 2018, Simon Benson, in what *The Australian* labelled an 'exclusive', wrote:

> Senior ministers including a member of Malcolm Turnbull's cabinet have launched an extraordinary attack on the Victorian judiciary, claiming it was advocating lighter sentences for terrorists as part of 'ideological experiments'.

Hunt was quoted at length in the article. 'Comments by senior members of the Victorian courts endorsing and embracing shorter sentences for terrorism offences are deeply concerning – deeply concerning,' he solemnly declared. Keen, naturally, to make political capital out of the issue, Hunt called on the Labor government of Victorian Premier Daniel Andrews to 'immediately reject such statements and sentiments'. 'The state courts should not be places for ideological experiments in the face of global and local threats from Islamic extremism that has led to such tragic losses,' Hunt was quoted as saying.

Hunt's colleague, Michael Sukkar, was quoted in the article as claiming that the Andrews Government's 'continued appointment of hard-left activist judges has come back to bite Victorians. Our judiciary should focus more on victims and the safety of our society, and less on the rights of terrorists who don't respect our society, its laws or our people'. And according to Tudge, 'Some of these judges are divorced from reality'; 'some judges seem more concerned about the terrorists than the safety of the community'.

Sadly, the intemperate and just plain wrong remarks of these politicians were not unique. They were comments made by three individuals who would be unlikely to darken the door of a court, except for the purpose perhaps of giving character evidence for a friend. But attacks on the judiciary are now a regular feature of the rhetoric of the populist right. Judges are seen to be members of the 'elites' and therefore 'out of touch' with 'ordinary people'. More on that later.

What was frightening in this case, and frightening is the operative word, was that members of the executive branch of government would make public commentary on a case that was currently before the court.

Before *The Australian* carried Benson's article on its front page, the Victorian Court of Appeal had heard argument in an appeal brought by the Commonwealth Director of Public Prosecutions arguing that a sentence imposed in a case involving terrorism offences was too lenient. The judges who heard the case – Chief Justice Marilyn Warren, Justice Mark Weinberg and Justice Stephen Kaye – had not handed down their decision when *The Australian* story broke.

By making such strident and critical remarks about sentencing practices in terrorism cases in Victoria, the clear impression created was that the three ministers were trying to put pressure on the judges as they deliberated on the case. The fact that *The Australian* published the story was equally troubling. The hearing convened by the judges three days after *The Australian*'s front page story was marked by a refusal of the ministers to attend the hearing and to unreservedly apologise to the court for the timing of their comments. When *The Australian*'s lawyers made a full apology, they claimed to be the messenger. Stephen Donaghue QC initially told the hearing that the ministers acted in good faith and they 'did it to participate in what [they] considered to be an important public discussion' about sentencing in terrorism cases.

Donaghue was instructed by his clients to say that the ministers 'did not intend to undermine public confidence in the courts … the remarks were made in good faith and in an attempt to discharge [their] duties'. How the attack on the judiciary and the political tone of the attack could be said to be part of the ministerial duties of Hunt, Tudge and Sukkar remains a mystery.

Justice Mark Weinberg tackled the issue of a lack of apology from the ministers. When he noted that he had not heard an apology, this drew the response from Donaghue, 'You have heard regret as to the choice of language.' Not the same thing, Justice Weinberg accurately observed.

As the hearing ground on, with three judges fuming about the position they had been put in by the ministers and *The Australian*, Donaghue said his 'instructions had evolved somewhat' and that now the three ministers agreed to retract 'hard-left activist judges', 'ideological experiments' and 'divorced from reality'. The court adjourned to contemplate whether or not the ministers would face contempt charges.

It took a week for the ministers to apologise fully. On 23 June 2018, Donaghue told the court his clients had watched the proceedings of the previous week and bothered to read the transcripts of the appeal on which the judges had been deliberating. 'We have realised we should have offered an unconditional apology to the court. We offer that apology now and unreservedly withdraw all comments. It's clear just how inaccurate our understanding was,' the ministers said in a statement read to the court by Donaghue. This was the end of the matter, with the court accepting the apology.

The political media caravan moved on but the damage to the rule of law was done. The independence of the judiciary, a bedrock principle of liberal democracy and a core liberal value, had been smashed in the most egregious fashion by the three ministers, and for that matter by the newspaper that published their remarks.

As Chief Justice Warren rightly said at the outset of the proceedings against the ministers, the court had been placed in an appalling position by this clearly intentional attack on Victoria's legal system. 'On the one hand, if we don't allow the appeal then we will be accused of engaging in an ideological experiment of being hard-left activist judges,' Chief Justice Warren said. 'On the other hand, if we increase the sentences, the respondents would be concerned that we were responding to the concerns raised by three senior commonwealth ministers.'[1] As a former judge said to this author, the young offenders in the case – a nineteen-year-old known as

MHK and twenty-year-old Sevdet Besim – will always wonder if the increase in their sentences that was eventually ordered by the court occurred because of the contemptuous conduct of three ministers and a sympathetic media outlet.

The 'Yarra Three' saga set a new low in the slide that has occurred in recent years with regard to support for the rule of law in Australia. Of course the two reasons it is one of the key liberal values is because adherence to the rule of law is designed to protect us from abuses of executive power and because it advances individual autonomy. In Australia, as overseas, the populist right is busy attacking the rule of law. It has proved such a potent political strategy that the so-called 'left of centre' forces such as the ALP have become equally culpable in undermining the rule of law.

Do not think for a moment that the rule of law is some technical term thrown about by lawyers. It is fundamental to a liberal democratic society. There is no better exposition of this point than that articulated by English former judge Tom Bingham, whose short and highly readable *The Rule of Law*, published in 2010, defines admirably just how crucial it is that we understand what is at stake when governments, politicians and the media undermine the independence of the judiciary and seek to trash fundamental fairness in their obsession with 'law and order'.

Tom Bingham's book was based on what became a famous lecture, given on 16 November 2006 at the Centre for Public Law, which is based at Cambridge University.[2] In the lecture, Lord Bingham of Cornhill, to give him his title, articulated a series of rules that he said go to make up what is meant by the rule of law. His speech and subsequent book took issue with the illiberal anti-terror laws introduced by the Labour government of Tony Blair but supported by most politicians and much of the media in the United Kingdom.

The phrase 'the rule of law', Lord Bingham rightly noted, was much abused. He quoted Judith Shklar, the Harvard political scientist, who once said that the phrase 'may well have become just another one of those self-congratulatory rhetorical devices that grace the public utterances of Anglo-American politicians'.[3] She has a point. Former British prime minister Tony Blair, one of the enthusiastic proponents of the illegal war in Iraq, saw himself as a 'rule of law' proponent. 'If we can establish and spread the values of liberty, the rule of law, human rights and an open society then that is in our national interests too. The spread of our values makes us safer,' said Blair in 1999.[4] Right-wing populists like Australia's Tony Abbott also invoke 'the rule of law' when it suits. He tweeted on 14 July 2018, in defence of the Catholic Church, 'In a country under the rule of law, being critical of a government policy should never be the catalyst for official investigation.'

But what 'the rule of law' really means, according to Lord Bingham, is 'that all persons and authorities within the state, whether public or private, should be bound by and entitled to the benefit of laws publicly and prospectively promulgated and publicly administered in the courts'.[5] While this might seem a motherhood statement if made in a liberal democratic country like Australia, when the definition is applied it is clear that the populist right's policies and attitudes represent a threat to the rule of law.

Lord Bingham's definition of the rule of law led him to the view 'that questions of legal right and liability should ordinarily be resolved by application of the law and not the exercise of discretion'. In other words, it is the courts that should decide the rights and duties of individuals and other entities in our society, not ministers and bureaucrats. This is because 'the broader and more loosely textured a discretion is, whether conferred on an official or a judge, the greater the scope for subjectivity and hence for arbitrariness, which is the antithesis of the rule of law'.[6] When applied to the decisions of Australia's current Immigration minister, Peter Dutton, Lord Bingham's point is manifested frequently.

In keeping with the contempt it holds for courts and independent decision makers, the populist right has been busy giving to ministers, bureaucrats and other officials – like the heads of security agencies and police services – enormous powers that can infringe the rights of individuals and which are not capable of being scrutinised by the courts.

In the area of immigration, successive governments, but particularly the current prime minister, Scott Morrison, when he held the Immigration portfolio, and Dutton, have sought to sideline the courts through investing themselves and the bureaucrats in their department with the power to revoke visas. The consequence of this abandonment of the rule of law has been extraordinary and the ways in which these sweeping powers are used or misused by Dutton are a case in point as to why abandoning the rule of law leads inevitably, to use Lord Bingham's phrase, to 'subjectivity' and 'arbitrariness'.

And yet, due to the never-ending 'war on terror' underwritten by the populist-right media's perpetual fear campaign and the political class's inability and unwillingness to stand behind the rule of the law, what would once have been thought to have been draconian legislation is now being supported by nearly all those who are legislators.

Take, for example, amendments to legislation made in 2014 to allow ASIO to ask the Attorney-General for permission to call an operation a 'special intelligence operation'. If the Attorney-General grants the request, then ASIO officers are immune from prosecution if they commit crimes and civil wrongs, with only a handful of exceptions that include murder, serious assaults, torture, a sex offence or significant damage or loss of property. This means ASIO officers can rough up individuals and cause injury so long as it is not serious, keep them falsely imprisoned, burgle, trespass and steal. No judicial approval is required and, with the exception of journalists, it is a crime for a person to reveal anything about the operation, irrespective of the physical and psychological harm done to them and their family or loved ones.

These amendments were part of a drive by the Abbott and Turnbull governments to update 'national security' laws, as are new laws introduced by the Abbott and Turnbull governments that allow for a minister to cancel a person's Australian citizenship 'if the Minister is satisfied that it would be contrary to the public interest for the person to remain' a citizen. And whoever is the federal Attorney-General can prevent a defendant and his or her lawyer in a criminal case from being able to elicit or view evidence if the Attorney-General thinks the disclosure of evidence 'is likely to prejudice national security'. This is such a broad phrase that it could be used, and no doubt has been and will be used, injudiciously by the politician who is Attorney-General. (The days when the Attorney-General was the first law officer of the nation and to some extent independent of the political process have sadly long gone.) That decision is not appealable, despite the fact that it can prejudice the case for a defendant in criminal and civil proceedings.

It is not only in the area of the 'war on terror' that examples abound of ministers, bureaucrats and law enforcement agencies being given broad powers to infringe the rights of individuals. It seems whenever there is an outcry about the 'law and order' issue of the day – terrorism, gangs, drugs at music festivals or anything else where the populist-right media determines there is a 'crisis' – discretionary powers are placed in the hands of officials so they get to play judge and jury.

Most notoriously this is seen in the misnamed 'anti-bikie' laws that have been adopted across the nation over the past decade, led by South Australia and followed by other states and territories, most recently in Tasmania. When introducing 'bikie gang' laws in that jurisdiction, state Minister for Police Michael Ferguson, a former federal Liberal member of parliament and a card-carrying member of the populist right, made the extraordinary claim that giving the courts powers would be dangerous and that his proposed law:

> does not give [the individuals targeted by police] any chance to drag this through court with injunctions and legal moves, adjournments, gathering of evidence, cross

> examination, questioning witnesses, going after people to suggest they are not fit to sit over a case, and vexatious claims that would drag this out for years and would only give the upper hand to the outlaw bikie gangs and their criminal defence lawyers.[7]

We also see the use of secret ministerial and bureaucratic processes when it comes to so-called 'working with vulnerable people' checks. The power of the minister responsible, or of her or his bureaucrats, to stop a person's employment or volunteer position with children, for example, is so broad as to include the mere existence of an allegation against that person. No matter if the allegation is patently false or has been fully investigated by police and found to have no veracity. In many cases a person's employment ceases and they suffer reputational damage, and when they are cleared they receive no compensation. Just grin and bear, that is the message.

Lord Bingham also argued that the rule of law means 'the laws of the land should apply equally to all, save to the extent that objective differences justify differentiation'.[8] That is, while children, prisoners and persons with mental illness can be treated in a different way because of their legal circumstances, we should otherwise not discriminate against anyone when it comes to the protection of the law. 'It would be comforting to treat this sub-rule as of antiquarian interest only,' Lord Bingham wrote. 'But it would be unrealistic, as the treatment of non-nationals here and elsewhere reveals,' he observed.[9] He was speaking about the mistreatment of asylum seekers and those targeted by anti-terror laws on the basis of their being Muslim.

In this country the populist right has no difficulty discriminating against asylum seekers when it comes to how the law of this land works. Asylum seekers are discriminated against in social security laws because their eligibility for payments is not subject to the same criteria as those applicable to citizens of Australia. The ban on indefinite detention, except in specific circumstances such as sex offenders (which is troubling enough), which applies to all who reside in Australia, does not apply to asylum seekers. The courts sadly agree with the legislators that detention on Nauru and Manus Island and on-shore is not imprisonment but administrative detention. We jail children of asylum seeker parents, something that we do not permit our law to allow except as a last resort for youth. Asylum seekers have severe restrictions placed on their legal right to work and right to access Medicare health benefits.

But it is not just asylum seekers that we discriminate against when it comes to applying the law. Indigenous Australians in the Northern Territory have been subjected to the so-called Northern Territory Intervention, a jack-booted and ill-considered response of the Howard Government, and continued by the ALP, which prevents, for example, the application of commonwealth racial discrimination legislation to those citizens of the territory who are subject to the Intervention.

Another of Lord Bingham's examples of what the rule of law means in a liberal democracy is, as he argued, that 'the rule of law must, surely, require legal protection of such human rights as, within that society, are seen as fundamental'.[10] The populist right has no interest in protecting fundamental human rights, with the exception of those that suit it, such as religious freedom and freedom of speech, although even in those contexts there is hypocrisy and selectivity.

Ask yourself this question. When have you heard, read or watched a member of the populist right champion human rights? The answer is, without any sense of exaggeration, never. In fact the term 'human rights' is only ever used with disparaging connotations. For the populist right, the idea of human rights being enshrined in law, whether by way of a human rights act or by being embedded in the Australian Constitution, is simply anathema and must be resisted at all costs. This is because the populist right does not believe in universal human rights. The idea that all individuals be treated equally – irrespective of what they have done, how they are perceived or who they are – is not housed within the DNA of the populist right. Instead they divide humanity, just as was fashionable among the nineteenth-century middle class, into deserving and undeserving cases. Asylum seekers are undeserving, so they have no rights. Persons who commit crimes or who are charged with criminal offences are undeserving, so they should be stripped of rights. Indigenous Australians, like asylum seekers, are 'The Other' and so there is no sense in which human rights ought to be accorded to them on the same footing as the white middle and working classes.

One of the most respected human rights scholars in the world, Philip Alston, an Australian and incidentally brother of Richard Alston who was Communications minister in the Howard Government, argues that the 'populist agenda that has made such dramatic inroads recently is often avowedly nationalistic, xenophobic, misogynistic, and explicitly antagonistic to all or much of the human rights agenda'.[11]

We see this disturbing trend reflected in the populist right's rhetoric in Australia on a daily – yes, daily – basis. *The Australian*'s Chris Kenny, writing on 4 May 2017 in yet another assault on former human rights commissioner Gillian Triggs, sneeringly referred to 'the human rights crowd'. And another poster child of the populist right, Peta Credlin, a former Abbott Government staffer, in *The Daily Telegraph* on 15 May 2016, labels those who argue for human rights protections as 'a barrage of human rights activists'. James Allan, an academic from the University of Queensland, complained to a no-doubt sympathetic Hungarian audience earlier this year about 'human rights brigades'.[12]

The populist right is implacably opposed to universal rights being reflected in a statutory form. This is, of course, the case in nations such as the United Kingdom, New Zealand, Canada and nations that are members of the European Union. It is also the case, to a limited extent, in the United States of America.

But the idea of an Australian human rights law horrifies the populist right, who are interested only in their own rights as privileged men and women. This conclusion emerges when one analyses the reasoning, such as it is, and the language of members of this group as they pontificate about the evils of the Australian Human Rights Commission, its former head Professor Triggs, the idea of a human rights law, and the idea that human rights should be universal.

The populist-right politicians and commentators are at pains to say they do believe in rights. But it is one particular right that obsesses the populist right: the right to freedom of speech. Andrew Bolt, who is portrayed as a martyr for the freedom of speech cause, once proposed that a fellow populist-right commentator, Janet Albrechtsen, who writes for *The Australian*, replace Professor Triggs as human rights commissioner. Why? Because, he argued on his blog on 7 December 2016, this 'is a job that badly needs someone who finally respects the most important human right of all'. And what would that right be? Ah, freedom of speech of course!

For the populist right, the rule of law and freedom of speech are not compatible. The populist right is outraged at the idea that some person, group or regulatory body should ever dare to even enquire, or threaten legal action, after one of their own has exercised his or her 'right' to freedom of speech.

In Bolt's case the decision by a number of Indigenous Australians, led by the late Pat Eatock, to challenge assertions made in his *Herald Sun* column 'that they were not genuinely Aboriginal and were pretending to be Aboriginal so they could access benefits that are available to Aboriginal people'(to quote the summary of the 2011 Federal Court judgement delivered by Justice Mordy Bromberg) has been used as a lightning rod by the populist right to argue for weakening racial discrimination protections. It was as though Eatock and her fellow plaintiffs had been utterly outrageous in asserting their rights under the law.

Similarly, when the late cartoonist Bill Leak drew a cartoon that many believed reinforced the stereotype of 'lazy drunken' Aboriginal men, there was outrage from the populist right that the Human Rights Commission, which has a statutory obligation to enforce human rights laws in this country, would dare to criticise Leak's drawing. Tim Blair, writing in *The Daily Telegraph* on 20 March 2017, accused the Human Rights Commission's then race discrimination commissioner Tim Soutphommasane of orchestrating 'pathetic Twitter temper tantrums' by encouraging 'people via Twitter to lodge complaints with the commission about Bill Leak's celebrated depiction of Aboriginal neglect'. What Soutphommasane was doing, and rightly so, was to invite complaints.

When the same-sex marriage debate of 2016–17 was made interminably long, mainly by the hard right of the Liberal Party seeking to resist the inevitable by pointing the gun at former prime minister Malcolm Turnbull, the populist right became very keen on human rights. But not the human rights of same-sex couples; only the rights of those who advocated *against* same-sex marriage, particularly the Christian lobby. Muslims who similarly opposed same-sex marriage were not given much airtime by Bolt on his Sky News program, but if you were a Catholic bishop or a young Christian woman then Bolt was your friend.

The shameless selectivity of the populist right about human rights was also evident when Peter Dutton – aided and abetted by the ALP and cross-benchers, and with notable exceptions such as Denison MP Andrew Wilkie and the Greens – enshrined in law the criminalisation of disclosures from detention centres. The law, passed in 2015 and since watered down, made it a criminal offence, punishable by up to two years' imprisonment, for anyone who worked at an immigration detention centre to disclose, without obtaining permission, 'protected information', this information being so broadly defined that it meant essentially anything that related to the detention centre. This law was a clear breach of fundamental human rights, and obviously so. The 'most important right', as Bolt had called it, of freedom of speech, was comprehensively undermined by this law. But despite this there was silence on the part of the populist right.

The shrieking indignant protests, on the one hand, about the right to offend Indigenous Australians and Muslims in the name of the cherished human right of freedom of speech but the silence, on the other hand, about a direct attack on freedom of speech by a darling of the populist right says it all, really.

Secrecy is, of course, the enemy of the rule of law. Quoting US judge Damon Keith, who in 2002 famously said of the Bush administration's obsession with secret hearings in terrorism cases that 'democracies die behind closed doors', Lord Bingham argued that 'adjudicative procedures provided by the state should be fair. The rule of law would seem to require no less'.[13] Courting controversy among the political class and the right-of-centre media, Lord Bingham chastised the rise of secrecy in the way in which citizens and others are dealt with by the law in the 'war on terror' era.

Lord Bingham cited the 'disturbing' trend of the 'growing categories of case outside the strictly criminal sphere in which Parliament has provided that the full case against a person, put before the adjudicator as a basis for decision, should not be disclosed to that person or to any legal representative authorised by that person to represent him'. 'Any process which denies knowledge to a person,' he observed in a restrained but firm critique, 'effectively, if not actually, accused of what is relied on against him, and thus denies him a fair opportunity to rebut it, must arouse acute disquiet.'[14]

While he was speaking and writing in the context of the United Kingdom, Lord Bingham's observation is equally apt in Australia. There are numerous examples, but perhaps none more egregious than those involving asylum seekers who are kept in immigration detention with no release date in sight because they are judged by ASIO to be a security risk.

In 2010 and 2011, ASIO issued adverse security assessments to over fifty individuals who had been found to be refugees. The vast majority of these people were Tamils from Sri Lanka. Despite the catastrophic consequences of the adverse assessment – indefinite detention – these individuals were kept in the dark about how and why that assessment had been made. The Kaldor Centre, a think tank at the University of New South Wales, described the process this way:

> Most of the refugees had no advance notice of the allegations against them before the adverse security assessment was made. At most, they may have had certain contentions put to them in the course of their ASIO interview. None received reasons or evidence for the adverse assessment, and attempts by their lawyers to gain confidential access through existing legal mechanisms were denied. The substance of the decisions could not be reviewed, 'contrary to basic principles of due process and natural justice'.[15]

Anti-terror laws in Australia are characterised, as noted earlier, by secrecy and a lack of transparency. Take, for example, control orders. A person as young as fourteen can be issued with an interim control order that will severely restrict every aspect of their life, and if they breach it they will end up in jail for up to five years. But the person does not even get a chance generally to find out why the order is made because it is on the say-so of the AFP. The hearing to obtain the interim order is generally what is called 'ex parte', which means the person whose life is about to be grossly disrupted knows nothing of what is about to happen to them.

Under the National Security Information legislation, evidence can be kept from defendants and their lawyers. The latter are required to have a national security clearance, which of course is itself a secret process in which there is no transparency and whereby the executive government can curtail the right of individuals to the counsel of their choice, another element of the rule of law.

It is not only in the domestic context that the populist right has driven the undermining of the rule of law in Australia. Lord Bingham noted that one of the key indicia of the rule of law is the proposition that 'the existing principle of the rule of law requires compliance by the state with its obligations in international law, the law which[,] whether deriving from treaty or international custom and practice[,] governs the conduct of nations'. He added,'I do not think this proposition is contentious.'[16] Sadly, in Australia, it is – very much so.

The populist right in Australia, along with its comrades internationally, is contemptuous of international law and of the architect and forum of international rules, the United Nations. Former prime minister Tony Abbott once said, of yet another

United Nations report excoriating Australia for its recidivist flouting of international law in the context of asylum seekers and human rights:

> I really think Australians are sick of being lectured to by the United Nations, particularly, particularly given that we have stopped the boats, and by stopping the boats, we have ended the deaths at sea.

These comments, made on 9 March 2015, reflect the view commonly held by the populist right, and many in the so-called centre, for that matter (for instance, the ALP), that because you stop people drowning it is acceptable to inflict physical and psychological abuse on those individuals who did not drown but are instead detained in immigration detention.

The populist right is hostile to the idea that Australia should comply with the international law obligations it has signed up to over the years because these clash with its nativist mindset. Peter Dutton, speaking on 25 July 2018 to a populist-right colleague, broadcaster Alan Jones, said Australia would not sign up to a United Nations agreement that made it clear that detention of asylum seekers should be a last resort. Dutton's answer was straight out of the Steve Bannon playbook:

> We're not going to sign any document that's not in our national interest and it's not in our national interest to sign our border protection policy over to the UN. We're not going to surrender our sovereignty – I'm not going to allow unelected bodies dictate to us, to the Australian people.

Joining a handful of countries such as Hungary, Poland, Austria, Israel and Switzerland (with the exception of Switzerland these are nations that have in recent times embraced nativism), Prime Minister Scott Morrison told the media on 22 November 2018 that he 'would never allow something to compromise our borders, I worked too hard to ensure that we weren't in that position'.

These comments from Abbott, Dutton and Morrison are examples of a trend described by one commentator as politcians 'tapping into the social dissonance attributed to international law and international society'. The populist-right media also fuels this notion that Australian sovereignty and compliance with international law obligations are incompatible.

And if Australia signs up to, and complies with, international law, then this amounts to a takeover of the nation, according to the populist-right argument. Maurice Newman, a former businessman and confidant of John Howard, wrote in *The Australian* on 8 June 2015 that 'before we laugh off the prospect of global government based in Geneva and sleepwalk into surrendering more of our national sovereignty in Paris [referring to the climate change agreement], we should wake up'. At stake, according to Newman, are 'our individual liberties and our children's economic future'.

This idea that compliance by Australia with international law obligations will lead to the death of liberal democracy is a common theme of the populist right. Janet Albrechtsen wrote for the Samuel Griffith Society, a conservative talking shop, about the dire threat for Australia that is international law. The world has an 'obsession with international law' – which might sound 'a little dramatic', she wrote – but 'think about the exponential growth of international law in the last 50 years'. Then she went on to warn, without any hint that she was being ironic:

> We've gone from governing relations between countries to dictating relations between people. We've gone from asserting fundamental civil and political rights to force-feeding countries on a fashionable diet of new-fangled economic, social and cultural rights. And what each of those means depends upon who happens to be sitting on the relevant committee on a particular day. In other words, your guess is as good as mine. At this rate, where will we be in 50 years time? One thing is clear – the western liberal democratic nation state will be neither democratic nor a nation state.[17]

Albrechtsen's rant was the stuff of fantasy, of course, with no recognition that it is those who sympathise with her view of the world who are undoing liberal values in Australia. But note the hostility of the populist right to the idea of international law and Australia's participation in it, together with obligations to maintain it, is based also on the loathing for 'The Other'. When Albrechtsen refers sneeringly to 'new-fangled' rights, what she means is that the idea of rights has developed from the traditional type reflected in the eighteenth-century ideal of liberalism.

One of the most relevant (because it is often breached) indicia of the rule of law described by Tom Bingham as 'what many would, with reason, regard as the core of the rule of law principle' is 'that ministers and public officers at all levels must exercise the powers conferred on them reasonably, in good faith, for the purpose for which the powers were conferred and without exceeding the limits of such powers'. As Lord Bingham observed:

> although the citizens of a democracy empower their representative institutions to make laws which, duly made, bind all to whom they apply, and it falls to the executive, the government of the day, to carry those laws into effect, nothing ordinarily authorises the executive to act otherwise than in strict accordance with those laws.

He rightly highlighted that 'the historic role of the courts' has of course been to check excesses of executive power.

It is this aspect of the rule of law that is under serious threat in Australia today. The populist right, as we noted earlier, regards judges and other judicial officers with contempt in the main. They are seen as 'out of touch', part of the 'elite'. The comment made by Tasmanian MP Michael Ferguson, referred to earlier, sums up the populist right's dismissal of the idea that ministers and bureaucrats should have an effective check on their power in the form of independent courts.

Members of the populist right regard courts as a nuisance or as tools of dreaded 'social engineering'. Courts get in the way of the law-and-order agendas so beloved of the populist right. And courts stop ministers from having their way when it comes to trampling on the rights of people deemed by the populist right to not deserve rights at all.

When it comes to the point Lord Bingham made about the core of the rule of law being ministers and their bureaucracies exercising their powers in good faith and without exceeding their powers, and having the courts as a real check on excesses by those ministers and their bureaucracies, there is no better illustration than the case of Immigration Minister Peter Dutton, the most powerful of ministers when it comes to playing judge, jury, policeman, and God with the lives of individuals.

CHAPTER 5

The Rise of the Right, Personified

When Minister for Immigration and Border Protection Peter Dutton was given control of a new ministry unique in terms of the scope of its powers and resources, as well as its capacity to trample on the already fragile liberties and freedoms Australians 'enjoy', the challenge to liberal values was lifted more than a notch or three.

From January 2017, Dutton became the man who controls a quartet of security and police agencies invested with extraordinary powers since Tampa and the post-9/11 'war on terror'. At the same time, independent scrutiny of their conduct and actions has been substantially reduced. Never before in the history of the Commonwealth had spies (ASIO), police (AFP) and the militarised protectors of the 'border' (Australian Border Force) all reported to one minister. The portfolio has the (yet again) Orwellian title of the Ministry for Home Affairs – a noticeably benign name for an organisation that can spy on, search, harass, arrest, detain and haul before the courts any one of us at any time, and can do so sometimes in secret.

The department's doublespeak is starkly obvious in its so-called 'Vision' – 'A secure Australia that is prosperous, open and united'; and its 'Mission' – to 'Work together with the trust of our partners and community to keep Australia safe and secure, and support a cohesive and united Australia open for global engagement'.

The idea for such a beast came from the United States of America and the United Kingdom, apparently. Neither nation is a beacon for liberal values these days, obsessed as they are with the 'war on terror' and border protection. But you can never be too careful – what with refugees wandering the globe looking for security and safety, and the 'threat' of terrorism routinely announced through a gullible media that takes at face value the word of politicians flanked by uniformed officers at media conferences. So Australia, slavishly following whatever the USA and the United Kingdom do when it comes to security and law enforcement, can now say 'me too'!

The enormity of the power wielded by Dutton and his department has been described by Anthony Bergin, a security expert at a Canberra-based think tank Australian Strategic Policy Institute (ASPI). 'Peter Dutton is now Australia's chief security officer,' wrote Bergin in an opinion article published in *The Australian Financial Review* on 21 December 2017. '[T]he secretary of the new department, Mike Pezzullo, has said he envisions Home Affairs will reach into just about every area of the Australian economy and society.'

The populist-right Manichaean view of the world sees domestic society through the prism of security. And security, once the domain of the military in a liberal democracy, is now part and parcel of 'daily human life: military, political, economic, societal, and environmental'.[1] Allied to this is the obsessive quest for power that appears to drive Dutton. The Manichaean world view, which Dutton shares with Pezzullo, has already seen this politician seek to make true on Pezzullo's boast that the Home Affairs portfolio will encroach on every aspect of Australian society.

Grabs for power by Dutton and his agency are always framed in a 'war footing' fashion. On 28 April 2018, *The Daily Telegraph* revealed that Pezzullo had written to his counterpart in the Department of Defence seeking a substantial increase in monitoring of Australian citizens through a new spy agency, the Australian Signals Directorate (ASD). According to the report, Pezzullo's letter said,

> onshore and offshore ... Further legislative reform could enable the Australian Signals Directorate to have a stronger role in support of the Home Affairs portfolio and our law enforcement efforts against online, cybercrime and cyber-enabled criminal threats facing Australia. Traditional law enforcement does not have the technical capacity to fully identify, detect and disrupt systemic transnational organised crime and is ordinarily limited to dependence on foreign partners.

And Dutton has argued that the threat of crime and terrorism is of such an overwhelming magnitude that he has proposed laws described by Cynthia Wong of ASPI as:

> [allowing] Australian law enforcement and security agencies to order technology companies and even individuals to do vaguely described 'acts or things' to facilitate access to your encrypted data and devices through newly created 'technical assistance' and 'technical capability' notices. Although officials would still need a warrant to obtain private communications and data, the bill requires no prior judicial authorisation before the attorney-general could compel your phone maker or app provider to undermine their security features.[2]

Wong has noted that 'the proposed law leaves too much discretion to officials to decide whether an order is justified as necessary and proportionate, and doesn't impose sufficient safeguards to prevent abuse'.

In a word, former police officer Dutton is a zealot. He sees the world, so his wife Kirilly said in a Fairfax Media *Good Weekend* profile, in black and white; there is no grey. It is called concrete thinking and it is the hallmark of many police officers around the nation.

Of course, Dutton dresses up his simplistic and therefore highly dubious world view in simple terms. He is the Good Cop and the morally upright citizen. In a speech he delivered on 10 October 2018 to the National Press Club, Dutton observed:

> In politics, and particularly as a Minister in a portfolio like this, you have a defined time to deliver on your priorities and I have always believed that the worst people in politics

> are those who can't or won't make decisions lest they offend one group or another. Those who don't know what they believe in and those who are too meek or weak to defend their values.

And then there was this statement – sanctimonious, self-congratulatory and alarmingly lacking in any sense of humility:

> I have given twenty-six years of public service, and protecting and keeping our community safe, women and children and vulnerable people safe, is a core value for me and I believe for our country. It doesn't always make you popular, but Australians know that I will fight to defend them and their families and to make our country a safer place.

This was not the only reference Dutton made in this National Press Club speech to his police officer past. He shamefully, but unsurprisingly, utilised it to send the message that it is vital he and his department not be stopped in their quest to rid Australia of criminal activity. 'In the early 1990s as a young detective I worked on a case of a young teenage girl who had been raped by a male offender who entered her home late one night,' Dutton told his audience.

> The victim's father was home asleep at the time but didn't hear the offender enter the house. Some more than twenty-five years on I can still remember the full name and dates of birth of both the victim and the offender. The offender was convicted and imprisoned, but I wonder from time to time what life would have been like or has been like for that young girl

> as she has grown up, and whether her father had ever got over the guilt of not waking to protect his daughter on that night.

A manipulative but effective story.

The speech also included an attack against the 'elites' – in this case, Silicon Valley companies.

> Now there are vocal opponents to this legislation, indeed some of the biggest critics of this legislation are multi-billion dollar Silicon Valley companies. The same companies that need to be hounded to pay tax in Australia and other jurisdictions, and the same companies who have misused personal data to commercial advantage. And it should be noted, these yes, are the same companies who protest about having to help police with the encryption problem, whilst operating their businesses in less democratic countries and accepting at the same time a compromise on privacy to allow their presence in those growth markets.

The fact that Silicon Valley companies are concerned about the broad sweep of powers Dutton seeks, including a lack of independent judicial oversight of the powers to demand data and cooperation from encrypted messaging hosts, was not even alluded to by the minister.

Like populist-right politicians across the world, Dutton sees himself as the saviour of Australian society from the 'forces of darkness'. Drug traffickers, paedophiles, fraudsters, terrorists (all of whom are protected or given soft treatment by the elites – that is, Silicon Valley, the judiciary and lawyers), you name it …

Dutton's message to the public is that you must trust him to keep you safe from these forces of evil and those who would stop him from doing so effectively.

Dutton's National Press Club speech fits within the observation by communications analysts that the language and style of populism is 'increased rhetorical appeal to "pathos" (emotional appeal) as opposed to substantive facts' and 'appeal to "the people" by claiming the moral high ground, subverting and undermining the establishment, and producing identity performances that signify closeness to "the people", as opposed to the perceived remoteness of mainstream political elites'.[3] Dutton's black-and-white and Manichaean world view is supported by Secretary Mike Pezzullo who once gave a bizarre speech essentially dividing the globalised world up into a simple 'forces of darkness and forces of light' scenario.[4]

It is worth reflecting for a moment on the inherent danger that lies in allowing Dutton to have accumulated so much power as both Minister for Immigration and Border Protection and now as Minister for Home Affairs. In the *Good Weekend* profile, written by Jane Cadzow and published on 23 May 2017, Dutton's wife expresses the view that the essence of her husband is his intellectual rigidity, not that she would use that phrase. But as an American writer, Byron Williams, observed in *The Huffington Post* on 10 February 2006:

> To see the world in black and white is to live within the contours of extremism. This outlook neatly divides the world into right versus wrong, good versus evil, and yes versus no. This thinking is dependent upon such words as

always and never. Especially in times of crisis, the black and white worldview is looked upon as strength and courage to the casual observer.

Dutton's zealotry and his simplistic outlook mean he should never be allowed near discretionary decision making of any consequence. Yet complexity is inherent in the nature of the decisions Dutton makes when it comes to immigration, border security, national security and the balancing between security and liberty.

But if Dutton is as his wife describes him, and no one appears to have cavilled with her proposition, then this makes Dutton unsuited for complex decision-making tasks. As American psychotherapist Dr Joseph Burgo puts it:

> Black-and-white thinking reflects the psychological process known as splitting. When we feel unable to tolerate the tension aroused by complexity, we 'resolve' that complexity by splitting it into two simplified and opposing parts, usually aligning ourselves with one of them and rejecting the other. As a result, we may feel a sort of comfort in believing we know something with absolute certainty; at the same time, we've over-simplified a complex issue.[5]

The black-and-white mindset of Dutton explains perhaps why he is so intolerant of, and contemptuous about, the checks and balances of liberal democracy despite his assurances to the contrary. In particular, Dutton appears to chafe at the role of the independent judiciary and the legal system in ensuring that power is not abused by the executive arm of government and particularly agencies such as Immigration officials, ASIO or the AFP.

Dutton's hostility to 'elites' and the idea that there should be strong constraints on his moral crusade on behalf of 'ordinary Australians' – hallmarks, as we noted earlier, of the populist right – manifests in what appears to be a visceral contempt for the rule of law. The idea that the law is available to everyone, irrespective of their station in life, and that the role of courts is to protect against abuses of power by ministers and their bureaucracies – sometimes called monitory democracy – is seemingly unimportant to Dutton. His attitude and his preparedness to act in a way that sidesteps courts and international law bodies, or treats their decisions with contempt, is nothing short of abuse of power.

As noted in a collaboration between *The Conversation* and the Sydney Democracy Network (the latter a global partnership of researchers, journalists, activists, policymakers and citizens concerned with the future of democracy):

> Public integrity bodies, human rights commissions, activist courts, participatory budgeting, teach-ins, digital media gate watching, global whistle-blowing, bio-regional assemblies: these and scores of other innovations were designed to check populists bent on self-aggrandisement in the name of 'the people'.

But, they write:

> populism is making a comeback, and that populism is indeed an autoimmune disease of monitory democracy. Populism

> picks fights with key monitory institutions, such as the courts, 'experts', 'fake news' platforms and other media 'prostitutes'. The new populism wants to turn back the clock to simpler times when (it imagines) democracy meant 'the people' were in charge of those who ruled over them.[6]

Dutton's conduct, rhetoric and beliefs fit within this characterisation quite neatly. Numerous examples abound. One that was extraordinary, if for no reasons other than tasteless politics and because of its cavalier approach to the taxpayers' pockets, was Dutton's response to a June 2017 settlement that required the Commonwealth to pay out $70 million to the men the Rudd Government transported from Australian immigration detention to Manus Island, a hellishly hot remote community off the Papua New Guinea coast, plus around $20 million dollars more in legal costs.

Dutton and his predecessor in the Immigration and Border Protection portfolio, Scott Morrison, owed a duty of care to this group of around 1900 men who, while on Manus Island, had been subjected to appalling treatment that harmed their physical and mental health. The case settled, after a lengthy fight between the Manus detainees, the Commonwealth and the contractors it engaged, Broadspectrum and Wilson Security. The court-sanctioned settlement of $70 million is large in any context in Australia, but this one was the largest in a human rights context, and it was the taxpayers of Australia who would foot a large part of the bill.

Dutton's reaction to the settlement, which was, of course, agreed to by the legal team acting for him and his department, was to accuse those lawyers who acted for these mentally and physically scarred falsely detained men[7] of being 'ambulance chasers' who had links to the ALP and unions. And of course Dutton maintained it was all the fault of the previous ALP government who put the men on Manus Island.

Dutton's populist-right rhetoric was equalled by the former prime minister, Tony Abbott, who said it was the fault of the courts. 'We've got a judiciary that takes the side of the so-called victim rather than the side of common sense,' Abbott said on 2GB before putting the boot into these desperate detainees by essentially accusing them of lying. When he was asked about the genuineness of the injuries suffered by the men, Abbott's extraordinary and evidence-free response was, 'I doubt it very much.' These responses were straight out of the populist-right playbook: You, the ordinary Australian, have had the wool pulled over your eyes by left-wing lawyers and judges, and, of course, these asylum seekers are dishonest. The fact that all the Victorian Supreme Court did in this case was approve a settlement agreed to by all parties, together with the fact that it was obvious Dutton and his department must have been told the government risked losing the case, was ignored by Dutton and Abbott.

The preparedness of Dutton to undermine the authority of the third arm of government – the courts – is a tactic of the populist right around the world. Courts, judges, magistrates and the lawyers who appear before them are 'out of touch' and 'left wing' and do not listen to 'the people'.

Dutton's routine attacks on the independence of the courts and tribunals in Australia also fit within the populist-right narrative. Andrew Arato, Professor of Political and Social Theory at the New School for Social Research, New York, outlines the narrative this way:

> By identifying the genuine people's will with its own, the populist leader or group inevitably sees the intervention of courts as linked to the secret work of an oligarchical enemy or the deep state or an external power. Once the will is incarnated, there is no reason to move to higher levels of legitimacy and to alternative procedures to test whether it is a genuine democratic will. Even the attempt to defend individual rights by courts becomes superfluous, because, the members of the authentic people supposedly need no rights against themselves, and their enemies must not be given rights to oppose the sovereign will.[8]

Keep this apt and cogent description of the mindset of the populist-right politician in considering Dutton's comments and interventions since he assumed the Migration portfolio in late 2014.

In the eight months from January to August 2018 alone, Dutton used no fewer than fourteen interviews to attack the courts and the Administrative Appeals Tribunal, which has the power to overturn the decisions of his department. In a 9 January interview with John MacKenzie on radio 4CA Cairns about the so-called 'African gang' crisis in Melbourne, Dutton accused lawyers of denying there was a crime wave: 'I don't understand why people within legal circles, within some parts of the community, want to deny that it's even taking place,' he told the sympathetic MacKenzie – or, as Dutton called him, 'Macca'.

And when MacKenzie put what was, without foundation, a suggestion from a police union that judges in Victoria were deliberately handing down sentences of less than twelve months to visa holders so Dutton couldn't cancel their visa as easily, the minister agreed with the notion:

> There are some instances where we have magistrates, judges, who are suggesting that they'll sentence for a period less than twelve months so that it doesn't trigger the deportation. I find that quite incredulous [*sic*] and I think the judiciary, frankly, needs to explain their position.

But, Macca of course said, 'the separation of powers provision applies at the federal level as it does at the state, I presume?' Dutton was quick to agree that was the case and 'rightly so'. He was not 'trying to lean on judges', the minister said. But:

> the judiciary is not above the Australian public. The public has an expectation that community standards will be met when sentences are passed down, when they're imposed on criminals who have committed serious offences and I think when the public asks those questions, to be fobbed off by some members of the judiciary is unacceptable.

And, said Dutton,

> [if] we're to have faith in the judiciary, as we should, then they need to provide that information to the public so that

> the public can have confidence because at the moment there are many people right across Australia who are quite disillusioned with the way in which some of these sentences are imposed.

There was no explanation as to how judges are 'fobbing off' the community, and no examples of sentences given, but the message was clear.

It is notable that Dutton denies attacking the independence of the judiciary. On 22 February 2018, in an interview with Sky News, Dutton thought his criticism of the judiciary would 'strengthen public faith because it's an incredibly important institution'. But he then proceeded to run through his 'sentences have to reflect community values' rhetoric, once again bereft of any examples of cases where that is *not* the case. Dutton wants to 'see a better reflection in some of the sentences of the public's attitude' because that will 'restore and help build that faith within [*sic*] the judiciary'.

It had, however, been in his first interview for 2018, on 25 January, on Sydney's 2GB with Ray Hadley, that Dutton's attacks on the judiciary took a seriously sinister turn. The interview included the following interchange between Hadley and Dutton.

> RAY HADLEY:
> While I was away, you were at odds with a Victorian judge because you correctly identified Sudanese gangs as terrorising people in parts of Melbourne. I note the judge's social media postings have been taken down after criticism of him about having the audacity to question you about what

you'd said, and people said what happens in the future if a matter like this comes before him, given that he appears to have a biased view in relation to Sudanese gangs …

You and I appeared on *A Current Affair* early this week talking about magistrates giving foreign criminals softer sentences.

Now I'm afraid that Queensland appears to be head and shoulders above the rest, particularly with a magistrate at Southport – I think she's still at Southport – named Joan White. Now Magistrate White appears to be a crusader politically for people who shouldn't be here. I have suggested on *A Current Affair* and I'll suggest now that what Magistrate Joan White should do is resign from the magistry [*sic*]. She should then offer herself for election in a Queensland state election or a federal election and then she can make changes if in fact she's elected to that position, which is a faint hope.

But I mean it really galls everyone when foreign criminals are given softer sentences to stop them being deported by your department.

PETER DUTTON:

Well, Ray, you're right. In terms of the way in which the Migration Act works – just to the benefit of your listeners – if somebody's sentenced to a twelve-month period of imprisonment then they can come within the character test under the Migration Act, which means that there is the ability to cancel their visa and on other grounds including if they're a child sex offender by way of another example, or a member of an outlaw motorcycle gang.

So what we've seen in a couple of cases – and one particular magistrate was talking about it in open court, so it's part of the transcript – was that if the magistrate sentenced this individual to twelve months or more, he faced deportation. So you're seeing sentences now where they're delivering softer sentences – less than twelve months – so that they don't get deported, and again I just think that's absurd, it's outrageous.

The job of the magistrate is not to be the local advocate for civil rights or for the prosecution for that matter. I mean their job is to impartially look at a matter and, in my judgement, to impose a penalty which reflects community standards. And the courts have the legislation there which has maximum penalties …

One of the most important things that an elected government can do – in this case the Labor Government in Queensland – is to appoint sensible people to the bench and if you're appointing civil libertarians and people that are political advocates – I mean Lex Lasry, the judge you just spoke about in Victoria tweeting to me – people need to question these appointments and I don't see that we shouldn't be able to point these issues out because if the Queensland State Government here, or in Victoria, or New South Wales, is making a decision to appoint civil libertarians and others to the benches of the Magistrate's Court and higher courts, and we're seeing softer sentences as a result, then the community should be outraged by that and I think they are outraged by it.

So this issue in relation to the magistrate on the Gold Coast is really one for [Queensland Premier] Annastacia Palaszczuk to answer and so far she's refused to answer any questions on it.

The clear inference from Dutton's response to his interviewer's editorialising was that appointments to the judiciary should be based on political outlook and that, when a magistrate or judge makes comments with which Dutton disagrees, then 'people need to question these appointments'. Here his target was a highly respected Victorian Supreme Court judge, since retired, who had dared to take issue with one of Dutton's evidence-free remarks about crime in Melbourne. According to Dutton, people are scared to go out to dinner because of fear of crime. Justice Lasry had remarked on Twitter: 'Breaking: there are citizens out to dinner in Mansfield tonight and they're not worried.' It was a humorous remark and not a remark involving any case currently before his court.

The attack on the Gold Coast magistrate by Dutton and Hadley was likewise underpinned, it seems, by a view that she should be removed from her position because she dared to take a view of a case that was different from the one that suited Dutton and Hadley.

But where Dutton's attacks on judges and magistrates are somewhat sporadic and opportunist, when it comes to the Administrative Appeals Tribunal, his attacks (along with those by News Limited and other media commentators such as Hadley) on its independence have become routine.

The AAT, as it is known, was established in 1975 and its role, as described on its website, is to 'conduct independent merits review of administrative decisions made under Commonwealth laws'.

Much of its work in recent years has been in the migration area. It deals with asylum seekers, people who are punished for criminal offences and who then have their visas revoked by Dutton and his department. In fact Dutton boasts that he has revoked the visas of, and deported, a record number of visa holders in the past four years: 'we have made Australians safer by cancelling the visas of more than 3800 dangerous criminals – including murderers, rapists and robbers – between December 2014 and August 2018,' Dutton told the National Press Club in his October 2018 speech.

Sometimes, as is meant to be the case with an independent review of decisions by Dutton and his bureaucrats, the AAT finds in favour of the person seeking asylum or the visa holder. This outrages Dutton, his department and the News Limited media. Since launching a major attack on the AAT in May 2017, Dutton has regularly undermined this inexpensive system of independent review of government decisions.

The problem is, says Dutton, that the AAT members, like judges, magistrates and lawyers, are not accountable to the community and they make political decisions – in other words, they are thoroughly unprofessional. Consider the following exchange with Ray Hadley on 18 May 2017.

> RAY HADLEY:
> Well, well, well, they're coming after you, the Admin Appeals Tribunal, you've been a naughty boy, you're in trouble with the Law Council of Australia. Have you lost sleep over that?
>
> PETER DUTTON:
> No, I think if you tell the truth you should sleep well at night and I think people, when they have a look at some

of these cases that are being decided by the AAT or in some of the courts, people who believe that they're above the law, above scrutiny by the public, I think should be the ones that shouldn't rest too well at night. If people are deciding matters and they aren't meeting community expectations then I don't see why people shouldn't face scrutiny over that.

RAY HADLEY:
Okay. Well it's almost side-splittingly funny that the Law Council President – whom I don't know – Fiona McLeod should say Tribunal members reviewed government decisions in accordance with law, not personal preference or ideology.

She must be on another planet, given – and I'm not talking about just this tribunal the AAT, I'm talking about magistrates, judges of all persuasions – if she thinks that they're [sic] background ... maybe she needs to have a good long look, Immigration Minister, at the Magistrate's Court at Southport to see exactly what the Labor-appointed magistrates do in that court among many courts across the country.

This exchange, like many others Dutton has with sympathetic media over the issue of courts and tribunals, is dripping with irony – not that he, and in this case Hadley, can see it. What they are arguing for is courts that succumb to their values and views, which, of course, they argue, like good populists everywhere, are the values of 'the people'.

Since Dutton, in the middle of 2017, launched his attack on the one body that regularly overturns his and his department's decisions, a search of his ministerial website shows that he has furthered his cause on no fewer than twenty-one occasions in media interviews.

The Australian, the *Herald Sun* and *The Daily Telegraph* have been strong supporters and advocates for Dutton on the issue of beating up on the AAT. On 22 May 2017 the *Herald Sun* ran a story with this headline: 'Administrative Appeals Tribunal saves scores of murderers, rapists, paedophiles from deportation'. Calling the AAT members 'bureaucrats', the *Daily Telegraph* ludicrously advocated that 'any time a murderer, rapist, paedophile, armed robber or drug dealer is knocked back for deportation by the AAT', meaning the AAT reversed the deportation order, 'that person is allowed to remain in Australia on only one condition – that he or she obtain a permanent dwelling no more than two properties away from an AAT bureaucrat's house'. *The Australian*, on 17 September 2017, headlined an anti-AAT story with this bizarre headline: 'Star chambers must not decide who enters Australia'. Bizarre because anyone with any familiarity with the relatively informal and open-to-the public-AAT knows that it is anything but a star chamber!

But it is not only the relentless hostility and critique that Dutton and his media allies engage in against the independent judiciary that astounds; it is also how Dutton makes decisions about the lives of individuals and what he does when courts take issue with that decision-making process.

One upon a time, when a court handed down a decision that was critical of a government minister, some respect was accorded that view. The government would say it was looking at the decision carefully and would respond in due course. Implicit in such a response was a respect for the rule of law on the part of the executive and certainly most who worked within it.

But, as we have noted, in Dutton such circumspection is hard to find. Dutton has, on at least two occasions within an unseemly short time period, overturned or rendered irrelevant successful court challenges to the exercise of his power to cancel a person's visa on the grounds of their criminal record.

An illustration of Dutton's capricious nature when it comes to courts insisting he conduct himself according to basic principles, like fairness, was illustrated in a judgement handed down on 24 July 2017 by the Full Court of the Federal Court – the second highest court in the federal hierarchy. Dutton had cancelled the visas of two men, Helder Carrascalao and Tomasi Taulahi, late on 14 December 2016. This was the second time he had done so, after being told by the Full Court of the Federal Court earlier that day – at 4.15 pm to be precise – that it was overturning his previous attempt to remove the two men from Australia. Carrascalao was born in East Timor, Taulahi in Tonga. They both had criminal records and were alleged to be associated with motorcycle gangs.

Dutton's zealotry got the better of him on the evening of 14 December 2016 and it was his conduct that night that landed him in trouble again with three judges of the Federal Court in July 2017. How Dutton responded to the overturning of his original decision to revoke the visas of Carrascalao and Taulahi is revealing and – if you believe that, in a liberal democracy, serious decisions affecting a person's fundamental rights should be made only after careful deliberation – frightening.

After the 4.15 pm decision there was a flurry of activity involving the Department of Immigration, Dutton's office and the lawyers for the two men. At 7.37 pm and 7.43 pm respectively, about 370 pages relating to Carrascalao and 300 pages concerning Taulahi were sent by the Department of Immigration to Dutton's office. Despite the voluminous nature of the material, which even at a cursory read would take more than an hour or so, Dutton made his decision to again cancel Taulahi's visa at 8.18 pm and Carrascalao's visa at 8.25 pm.

While the Federal Court judges Edward Griffith, Richard White and Robert Bromwich could not determine how long Dutton spent on each submission, they forensically analysed just how little time Dutton actually read and mulled over each of the cases. What was clear, the judges said, was 'that, assuming a five minute delay in providing hard copies of the material to the Minister after they were received electronically by his personal staff, the Minister had, at most, thirty minutes to consider all the Taulahi material'. And:

> [a]ssuming that he was unable to turn his attention to the Carrascalao material (in either its original or revised form) during that period, he had, at most, thirteen minutes to consider the relevant material before he decided at 8:25 pm to cancel Mr Carrascalao's visa (i.e. the six minute period between 7:42 pm when, on the stated assumption, hard copies of the original Carrascalao material were placed before the Minister until 7:48 pm when, on the same assumption, the Taulahi

> material was placed before him, and the seven minute period between 8:18 pm to 8:25 pm, being the interval between the finalisation of the two visa cancellation decisions).

Not surprisingly, the judges said forty-three minutes represented 'an insufficient time for the Minister to have engaged in the active intellectual process which the law required of him in respect of both the cases which were before him'.

Dutton's statements of reasons for signing in relation to both men that December night, the judges said, were 'replete with statements to the effect that the Minister had noted, found, accepted, had regard to, considered and recognised particular matters. These should not be understood as mere verbal formulae'. Instead they 'should signify that the Minister had engaged intellectually with each particular matter and had positively formed the state of mind which each conveys. It is reasonable to suppose that the formation of these multiple states of mind would occupy a Minister for some considerable time.' 'On the timelines outlined earlier, that does not seem to have been possible in the present case,' the judges concluded.

This case was not the only one in which Dutton appeared to take little note of court decisions that have dealt extensively with how he exercises his powers. In fact, only a few weeks after his humiliation at the hands of the Federal Court, Dutton dealt just as swiftly with a High Court challenge by another visa holder, AJ Graham, who had been a bikie gang member and who Dutton wanted to send back to New Zealand.

When the High Court delivers a judgement, most parties take time to consider it carefully. Not Dutton. On 6 September

2017, within an hour of the court handing down a decision overturning the Immigration Minister's use of secret information to cancel Graham's visa, Dutton cancelled the visa again. As in the cases of Taulahi and Carrascalao, Dutton had already responded to a previous court decision in Graham's favour by revoking his visa within hours of that court's decision in 2016. The High Court decision was lengthy and complex, dealing with the use of secret information to revoke a person's visa. In this case Dutton used a secret dossier of information on Graham as a primary reason for revoking his visa.

But Dutton and his department were not going to take the time to consider the High Court's lengthy and complex judgement. Within an hour of the decision, the minister had revoked Graham's visa yet again. This time Graham, having been housed inexplicably in the notorious Goulburn supermax prison for much of his time in immigration detention, was deported from Australia.

Professor Andrew Arato's observations about the populist leader 'identifying the genuine people's will with its own' and seeing 'the intervention of courts as linked to the secret work of an oligarchical enemy or the deep state or an external power' are apt in Dutton's case. More than any other member of the executive, Dutton, in his attacks on courts and tribunals, has presented himself as the 'people's voice' and judicial officers as believing they are beyond or above 'the people'. In other words, the latter is the dark force undermining the community.

If Dutton were a lone voice or a maverick MP, then to say that his illiberal approach was of a threatening nature, in terms of liberal democracy, would be an exaggeration. But he is not a lone voice or a maverick MP. In 2018 he nearly became prime minister, and the largest news organisations in Australia support him and his illiberal outlook. This is not a one-person crusade. Dutton's populist-right demeanour is reflected throughout Australia in outlets such as Sky News – after 6 pm, as they say, when its monotonous populist-right commentators take to the screen – and in much of the Australian electronic and print media.

Veteran broadcaster and journalist Stan Grant, writing in the immediate aftermath of Dutton's failed run at the prime ministership in August 2018, observed:

> Opinion polls show he may not be popular with the public, but that does not mean the issues [Dutton] champions are not resonating. He built his campaign around what he and others have identified as a change in Australian politics; it is a shift that aligns with the ideological battles that have so profoundly reshaped global politics.

Pointing to the variety of indicators showing that Australia is becoming less equal, and recent research showing 'Australia was among those countries losing faith in institutions', Grant insightfully observed of Dutton that, while 'his leadership ambitions have been thwarted, [...] the issues that have fired his campaign remain' and that Australia is 'not immune to the winds of politics blowing through our world'.[9]

While Dutton is not the only populist-right politician in Australia, in his rhetoric and approach to decision making it is certainly arguable that Dutton is emulating the emerging neo-fascist tendencies manifesting themselves in democracies today. James McDougall, Associate Professor of Modern History at Oxford University, says fascism is characterised by 'theatrical machismo, the man or woman "of the people" image', 'and the deliberately provocative, demagogic sloganeering that impatiently sweeps aside rational, evidence-based argument and the rule-bound negotiation of different perspectives – the substance of democracy, in other words – is only the outward form that this style of politics takes'. Writing for *The Conversation* on 16 November 2016, Professor McDougall goes on to observe,

> Fascism brings a masculinist, xenophobic nationalism that claims to 'put the people first' while turning them against one another. That is complemented by anti-cosmopolitanism and anti-intellectualism. It denounces global capitalism, blaming ordinary people's woes on an alien 'plutocracy' in a language that is both implicitly anti-Semitic and explicitly anti-immigrant, while offering no real alternative economics.[10]

Dutton is not anti-capitalist and he is not anti-Semitic, but he does use xenophobic nationalism as a rhetorical tool. He has contempt, as noted above, for an independent judiciary, and for non-government organisations and other critics in civil society. Secrecy is the hallmark of how he runs his portfolio.

On NGOs, Dutton, like his successor in the Immigration portfolio, Scott Morrison, is more than happy to smear when it suits. In 2014, Morrison falsely accused workers from the Save the Children Fund of 'allegedly coaching self-harm', adding that 'using children in protests is unacceptable, whatever their political views or agendas'. They didn't, as the evidence showed, but Morrison refused to apologise. Dutton, in 2016, accused the same NGO of leaking incident reports concerning mistreatment of asylum seekers on Nauru. Once again, there was no evidence to support the claim.

Dutton also sides with the European politicians who today are peddling the populist line about asylum seekers and borders. In a radio interview on 9 August 2018, Dutton observed that he would not be signing a UN global compact for migration, designed to deal with migration in a 'safe, orderly and regular' way.

> People see the scenes playing out on the Mediterranean or in Europe now, and our country, under this government, is not going to surrender our sovereignty, the protection of our borders, the protection of our society and we will not sign any agreement that would compromise that.

Hostility towards the UN, globalist solutions to people movement, and fears about losing a way of life are beliefs held by authoritarians in European nations such as France and Germany, in the Nordic countries and in the United Kingdom.

While Dutton might protest the characterisation of his fitting within the European neo-fascist and authoritarian movement today, he fits neatly into what is being observed by Stan Grant among others throughout the democratic world at the moment: the rise of intolerant, simplistic and nationalist politics. Dutton is a dangerous politician who represents a threat to liberalism.

CHAPTER 6

The Real Danger of the Populist Right

In a society in which liberal values are broadly cherished, there is room for civil disagreement and choices to be made, particularly when it comes to issues concerning the identity of the society. Australia Day is one such issue. How a community debate over Australia Day has been dealt with by the populist right, and why it represents an opportunity to reassert liberal values, is illustrative of what is at stake in Australian democracy.

In recent times many in our community have questioned the appropriateness of celebrating the nation that is Australia on 26 January, given that this day represents for Indigenous Australians the commencement of an invasive process by Europeans in their ancient land. The response by the populist right to those who have questioned whether another day in the calendar might better reflect inclusiveness, diversity and history has been patently illiberal. The threats from the Coalition government federally and the abuse meted out to those who argue to change Australia's national day have been depressingly familiar to those who long for an Australia where it is unremarkable – because it is the nature of a well-functioning liberal democracy – for such a debate to occur and for a new direction to be taken by the community.

In mid 2017, Sue Hickey, then lord mayor of Hobart (now the Speaker of Tasmania's House of Assembly), argued that there should be a discussion about moving away from 26 January as Australia's national day. For local government, Australia Day is of some significance because these councils hold citizenship ceremonies and receive Commonwealth funding for those and other activities. Hickey took her views to the Australian Local Government Association's national assembly in Canberra. The Hobart Council motion, 'that the National General Assembly encourage Australian councils to consider efforts they could take to lobby the Federal Government to change the date of recognition of Australia Day', won the day by two votes. 'This is history making,' Hickey said.[1]

Hickey's argument for considering the change was that it reflects reality in the Australian community. A month after the Canberra meeting Hickey told the media, 'There is growing acknowledgment that 26 January is not a day of celebration for all Australians.' She pointed out that '[e]very year there are public rallies, with people protesting against the current legislated date for Australia Day because Aboriginal people view it as invasion day. In Melbourne this year, 50,000 people – both indigenous and non-indigenous – protested'.

Hobart Council was not alone in its push to change the date. Other local governments have also voiced their concern about the fact that Australia Day is increasingly contentious for many in the community. On 25 August 2017, *The Australian* reported that nine councils, from Victoria, Tasmania and Western Australia, had begun discussions about changing the date of Australia Day. These councils were from across the political spectrum.

But the reaction from the populist right, in the form of the Turnbull Government and backbenchers such as Tasmanian Liberal Eric Abetz, to this activity from local government was, and remains today, swift and bullying and it reeks of intolerance of dissent. On 15 August 2017, Alex Hawke, the minister responsible for citizenship, had given an interview to News Limited's Renee Viellaris that was decidedly illiberal. After the interview, Viellaris wrote:

> Assistant Minister for Immigration and Border Protection Alex Hawke will today write to all 547 councils across Australia to warn them that if they test the Government with 'politically motivated public attacks on Australia Day', they will be punished.

Without, it seems, any sense of irony and not tongue in cheek, Hawke told Viellaris,

> The Australian Government will not allow council to politicise and delegitimise citizenship ceremonies in a public attack on Australia Day being held on January 26. If councils want to … fight an ideological war against Australia Day instead of … delivering value for ratepayers, that is their business, but they must leave Australian citizenship ceremonies out of it.[2]

In October 2017 a Greens councillor in Brisbane made statements at a Diwali Festival event about a citizenship ceremony taking place on 'stolen land'. Hawke claimed that the councillor, Jonathan Sri, had suggested that the Immigration Department and Australian Government 'has implemented costly and complicated processes, which make it difficult to obtain citizenship and for people to bring family members to Australia, and that this is motivated by racism and xenophobia'. Hawke was so incensed that he invoked a non-enforceable code of conduct for citizenship ceremonies that was designed to prevent political statements, and he threatened to strip Sri of his authority as a councillor to participate in citizenship events.[3]

Hawke's statements and threats have since been echoed by populist-right commentators and politicians across Australia. Naturally, the populist-right poster boy Andrew Bolt had to weigh in on the debate. Speaking on the eve of Australia Day 2018, Bolt told Chris Smith on Brisbane radio station 4BC that the debate about Australia Day had been 'hostile'. 'It's been absolutely and terribly divisive.' And of course, just to add to the divisiveness and hostility (again note the complete inability of a populist-right commentator to reflect on the irony of their position), Bolt blamed the 'cultural elites' who get a 'chance to disparage Australia, to say what's wrong with it'.

The Sydney broadcaster Alan Jones told Channel 7 on 16 August 2017 that the councils pushing for change were 'rat bags' – 'I mean there's four Greens, two Labors and a commie [*sic*]' – adding: 'these councils have no entitlement to determine when the national day is. They're irrelevant. It's a bit of a joke if it weren't so serious.'

Populist abuse and intolerance on the question of Australia Day was perhaps most fervently demonstrated by the News Limited columnist Peta Credlin, who used her *Daily Telegraph* column of 27 January 2018 to pronounce, in capitals, 'ENOUGH'. According to Credlin, the idea that Australia Day might not be set in stone was just too much. 'We've had it with the sneering campaigns, the moral superiority, the rewritten history and the attempts to make us ashamed for who we are and our place in the world,' Credlin fumed.

Then this potted history of European Australia:

> Australia was settled as a British penal colony, on lands inhabited by indigenous peoples, and is now one of the most diverse multicultural nations on earth. It is a fact – get over it.

Except, of course, it wasn't just 'inhabited'. Credlin appears to have forgotten the concept of Native Title. And then this advice for any Australian who doesn't get with the program: 'This is the best country on Earth; if you don't think so, buy yourself a plane ticket and head overseas.' According to Credlin, a discussion over an important symbol like Australia Day is just another 'obsession' of the left because they are emboldened by the success of the marriage equality campaign.

Credlin's remarks and the others cited above are manifestations of the illiberal fundamentalism that has taken hold in Australia since the late 1990s or the John Howard–sanctioned rise of Pauline Hanson and what she and her cohort represent.

What is paramount in these examples of the populist-right argument on any – and yes, it is any – discussion about moving Australia Day is that the discussion borders on treachery. As observed earlier, for the populist right, nationalism is a potent weapon and they view any attempts to question its totems, such as Anzac Day or Australia Day, as being a leftist exercise in undermining the nation.

The language of those who are seeking to at least examine whether Australia in the twenty-first century can do better than keep as its national day a date that is inherently problematic for Indigenous peoples and for many who value social cohesion and tolerance of 'The Other' has for the most part been reasonable and couched as a reflection of community discourse. By contrast, the language of the populist right has been abusive and hysterical – Credlin's rant being a case in point.

But debates about symbols like a country's national day, along with its other celebrations and reflections of significant events, are important and they should, in a liberal democracy, always be welcomed. Of course, the difficulty with the Australia Day debate and the populist right's reaction to it exemplifies what the populist right calls the 'culture wars'. The use of an aggressive term such as 'wars' is deliberate and it means that there can be no giving of ground by entrenched positions. 'Culture wars' is a construct utilised by the populist right to demonise opposition and to impose an intolerant brand of discourse on the issue – yet again ironically, given that it is the populist right that is obsessed by the idea of what it terms a fight against 'political correctness'.

To go to war implies there has to be a suspension of openness and tolerances, or the possibility of a new narrative or understanding of a symbol, an idea or a way of looking at a policy. The siege mentality kicks in and unwavering hostility to a supposed enemy is the order of the day. Liberal values and fighting wars don't go well together.

David Sergeant, writing in one of the right's favourite outlets, *The Spectator Australia*, actually thinks that there is not a 'war' but instead a 'massacre'. According to Sergeant, writing on 10 July 2017, 'it is more accurate to talk about a cultural massacre' because 'the left work[s] tirelessly and effectively to dominate every inch of our societal fabric'. There is, he feverishly maintains, 'an urgent choice':

> We can continue to offer economic liberalism and cultural Marxism lite or, we can be radical, unapologetic activists for our faith[,] our families and our communities. To do this, we must acknowledge leftist cultural domination … and counter it through a combative, radical vision and meaningful policy.

The 'culture wars' soldier sees the world very simply: there are 'cultural Marxists' (no one ever points to the theoretical link to Marxism, with its emphasis on class struggle, but let's leave it for the moment) who believe in multiculturalism, gender neutrality and atheism, and – worst of all – are not proud and unquestioning nationalists. Against them are the 'ordinary' Australians and their protectors who believe unwaveringly in what they perceive as traditional institutions such as family (mum, dad and heterosexual kids), a European view of Australian history, the superiority of Western civilisation, and strong borders.

Institutions that tolerate – or, worse still, propagate – openness and liberal values such as the education system, from primary schools to universities, and of course the ABC, are to be relentlessly assaulted and brought to heel by the populist right. After all this is a 'war' – or, if you believe Sergeant, a massacre – that must be halted. Whenever a populist-right warrior or shibboleth is rejected or attacked, irrespective of the reason, it is seen as another example of the 'Marxists' seeking to control the national agenda and the destiny of Australia.

One of the iconic culture war fights relates to a proposed centre being promoted by former prime minister John Howard (a veritable general for the populist right in the 'culture wars') that is designed to promote Western civilisation. The proposed 'Ramsay Centre' is to be, in the words of one of the primary architects of the 'culture wars', Tony Abbott, 'not merely *about* western civilisation but *in favour of* it'. Abbott, in an April 2018 essay in the monthly journal *Quadrant*, set out the remit of the Ramsay Centre as a weapon in the 'culture wars' and an active recruiter of minds within a particular university (at that stage it was the Australian National University, but now the mooted home is Sydney University).

According to Abbott, the fact that the centre 'is "for" the cultural inheritance of countries such as ours, rather than just interested in it, makes it distinctive'. 'The fact that respect for our heritage has largely been absent for at least a generation in our premier teaching and academic institutions makes the Ramsay Centre not just timely but necessary. This is an important national project,' he wrote. Referring to his own institutional mentors and inverting a concept coined by German student activist Rudi Dutschke, Abbott concluded:

> What an exhilarating prospect that upwards of a hundred bright young Australians every year might soon gain such inspiration. Person by person, the world does change. A much more invigorating long march through our institutions may be about to begin!

In other words, the role of the Ramsay Centre is to recruit to the cause of the 'culture wars' students who will then proselytise in favour of 'traditional values' and against the 'cultural Marxists'. Tony Walker, a veteran political and foreign correspondent, writing about the failure of the Ramsay Centre and the ANU to come to an agreement last year, rightly observed that 'an impression lingers that members of the Ramsay board were less interested in the study of Western civilisation than [in] its deployment in the endless culture wars that contribute little to [a] country's wellbeing'.[4]

The 'culture wars' are a sinister force when it comes to liberal values. And this manifests itself in the authoritarian stance taken by the populist right against the public broadcaster, the ABC. As we observed earlier, the ABC is seen as a bitter enemy of the populist right and, in fact, it needs to be controlled, brought to heel, and to serve the interests of the government of the day. To recall Abbott's chilling remark, the ABC seems to be on the side of everyone except Australia.

For those who are obsessed with the 'culture wars', the ABC, in all its manifestations, is the evil empire, stacked with

Marxists and soft liberals and committed to destroying the right. It does not matter – as the level-headed and rational doyen of political journalists in Australia, Michelle Grattan, has written – that while the ABC's enemies (in News Limited, and among Coalition, ALP and other conservative politicians) obsess over 'bias', they ignore 'that the perception of "bias" mostly varies according to where you're coming from, and [that] in journalism the notion of giving diverse viewpoints a fair go can be a more manageable one'.[5]

As mentioned, the 'culture wars' are never ending. Miranda Devine, writing in her *Daily Telegraph* column on 17 April 2018, set out the case for the manufactured war continuing forever and a day. 'Conservatives are sick of Coalition governments which appease the Left, curl into a ball and try not to cause outrage while Labor–Green governments remake the culture in their own image,' she wrote. Panic stations!

> The result is that the cultural Left has encroached on every aspect of our lives, from the relentless push to change Australia Day to the gender-neutral birth certificates proposed by the Queensland government. From corporations paralysed by 'diversity and inclusion', to Christians hounded out of the public square. From the promotion of Islam in school religion classes to the feminist-themed, virtue-signalling Commonwealth Games closing ceremony which emptied the stadium in record time.

'The left's "long march" through the institutions that Italian Marxist Antonio Gramsci once dreamt of has been a raging success,' Devine fretted.

On and on it goes. Relentless finger pointing, sledging and table thumping from the populist right until it gets its way. And its way would be a decidedly right-of-centre ABC news and current affairs outfit, abolition of human rights bodies like the one Gillian Triggs so effectively led, and an education system that allows for discrimination, religious teaching in state schools, and a triumphalist narrative around the nation that is Australia.

Alongside, and in fact a component of, the 'culture wars', is the divide created by the populist right between regional and suburban white Australians on the one hand and the so-called 'elites' who live in the inner suburbs. In this simplistic world, and manifest in the response of the populist right to the Australia Day debate, there are educated elitists who gather their news from the ABC, *The Guardian*, Fairfax media and an education system that is captive to them. Against this group are the genuine, 'ordinary Australians' who are spoken for by News Limited, Ray Hadley and other populist-right commentators. Home to these 'ordinary' Australians are the suburbs and the regions.

This division is reflected in Credlin's remarks about the Australia Day debate. It becomes an article of faith for the populist right that they speak for the 'real' Australians.

Paul Murray, one of the Sky News 'after 6 pm' brigade, used this simplistic division to castigate former prime minister Malcolm Turnbull who appeared on ABC TV's *Q&A* program on 5 November, Melbourne Cup eve, three months after he lost the keys to The Lodge. According to Murray, writing in his column in News Limited newspapers across Australia the day before, 4 November 2018, while Turnbull appears on *Q&A*,

Prime Minister Scott Morrison would be appearing with Murray on his program in Townsville. 'This was an opportunity I personally offered to Turnbull when he was PM last year, but he chose to ignore those people,' said the obviously miffed Murray. According to Murray, 'Morrison deserves credit, not because he's coming on Sky News, but because he wants to look Townsville locals in the eye.' It is Murray and Sky News that really 'cares' about Australians, according to Murray; 'The media will play their favourites, but you be the judge of who really cares about you,' he wrote.

Note the language of division here. While left-wing populists and those on the right both claim to be the genuine voice of the people, the difference is that – as observed by Peter Bloom, a senior lecturer in Organisation Studies in the United Kingdom's Open University – the former champion 'greater inclusion' and 'are plainly very different from right-wing ones keen on reinforced or increased exclusion'.[6]

The manufactured division between Australians, a daily exercise for the populist right, is corrosive of democracy. Paul Murray's comments above illustrate this point. To infer, as Murray seems to do, that there is a hierarchy of media audiences, and that a politician is to be chided because he does not take up an invitation to address a select audience in regional Australia as opposed to appearing on the national broadcaster, is unhelpful to say the least.

Murray is, of course, not Robinson Crusoe in his segmenting of Australian society. Judith Sloan, a columnist with *The Australian* newspaper, writing about the issue of what populism means, sarcastically referred to those who are opposed to Donald

Trump, Brexit and Pauline Hanson as being 'main chancers [who] live within the political beltway, sipping their organic chai lattes, largely immune from the daily pressures that affect ordinary folk'. News Limited columnist Piers Akerman lauded the newly minted Prime Minister Scott Morrison for a speech made in early September 2018 thus:

> Morrison is now appealing to the same strata of society, ordinary Australians, with the same core basic family values that swung the women's vote – in the face of sneering from the media and social elites who view basic family values as attributes of the 'reactionary Right.[7]

The populist right's division of Australians is not only unhelpful in building social cohesion but breathtakingly hypocritical given that it purports to be opposed to the latest derogatory label given to policy positions and politics with which it does not agree. That label is 'identity politics'. American scholar Francis Fukuyama has observed that politics these days is

> defined less by economic or ideological concerns than by questions of identity. Now, in many democracies, the left focuses less on creating broad economic equality and more on promoting the interests of a wide variety of marginalized groups, such as ethnic minorities, immigrants and refugees, women, and LGBT people. The right, meanwhile, has redefined its core mission as the patriotic protection of traditional national identity, which is often explicitly connected to race, ethnicity, or religion.[8]

For the populist right in Australia, 'identity politics' means a focus on groups and individuals who are not white 'battlers' or middle class. Miranda Devine claims that the ALP is pursuing what she terms 'the menace' of 'identity politics' because she counted up all the mentions in a draft party platform which she says are 'the language of identity politics and the rainbow agenda, almost to the exclusion of its traditional party values'. 'Lesbian', 'gay', 'gender' and such words were the subject of Devine's ire in a *Daily Telegraph* column of 30 October 2018.

The ABC of course comes under fire from the populist right because of its laudable liberal commitment to reflecting the diversity of the community in which it operates by favouring presenters who are not white, pale, male and stale. Andrew Bolt, writing in the *Herald Sun*, has fulminated about the ABC and the evils of 'identity politics' numerous times over the past two years.

So once again the populist right divides the community by sneering at efforts to cast aside labelling that perpetuates stereotypes – sometimes, it has to be said, overegged but at least well intentioned – by institutions like the ABC, the education system and governments.

The hypocrisy of the populist right types like Devine and Bolt is that they, too, indulge in identity politics. When Bolt, Devine and others in the populist-right camp devote column inches and airtime on Sky News to talking about white Australians being discriminated against, traditional families being under siege from 'anti-family radicals', or religious types who opposed the introduction of same-sex marriage being wrongly criticised or lampooned even for their stance, or when they defend US President Donald Trump and his support base, they too are indulging in identity politics.

In fact, as *The Economist* noted on 1 November 2018 in a comment on the recent US midterm elections, while in 'the popular imagination, identity politics is the stuff of queer-studies seminars and Hillary Clinton rallies' and the 'excesses of intolerant university students raging against misogyny, racism and homophobia have been rigorously catalogued', the reality is that '[r]ather less attention has been paid to the appetite for a different kind of identity politics – one centred around whiteness and championed by President Donald Trump. This kind of right-leaning identity politics is more potent than the left-leaning version'.

The newspaper's correspondent might equally have made the same observation about Australia. The populist right's obsessions with its apparently 'under siege' conservatives and their institutions are apparently all fine, but when someone stands for intersex, gay or transgender rights, the shrieks and sneering from the very same populist right become deafening.

It's a bleak picture. And made more so by the dominance in Australia of a handful of news organisations, and the potent success of scare politics and the politics of division that the Liberal Party has been so successful in executing since John Howard's 'battlers' election win of 1996. So much that the supposed centre-left force of the ALP now participates in populist-right gestures and is too frightened to assert liberal values.

It is sometimes said that, unlike the United States of America and parts of Europe, Australia does not need to fear the populist-right takeover of mainstream political parties; that individuals like Pauline Hanson, her new sidekick former Labor leader Mark Latham and their media friends are appealing to a *base* of voters but not the great middle. But this statement and this view are simply wrong. As we have seen in this book, the rhetoric, policy settings and so-called 'mainstream media' are infected with the populist-right bug to such an extent that liberal values in Australia are undermined on a daily basis. John Hewson, a former leader of the federal Liberal Party (1990–1994) and one of the few genuine liberals writing and commentating regularly in the Australian media today, rightly observed in his weekly Fairfax Media column on 8 November 2018 about the populist right's Number One hero, US President Donald Trump, that

> some of our politicians, beyond One Nation, have been tempted by his strong-man style, emulated his concern about political correctness, echoed him on 'media bias', envied his nationalism, and embraced his anti-immigration (including anti-Muslim) prescriptions and ill-considered gestures such as abandoning the Paris Climate Agreement and moving the Israeli Embassy from Tel Aviv to Jerusalem.

Hewson points to the extraordinary decision by coalition MPs to vote with Senator Hanson's October 2018 effort to have the Senate pass a white supremacist motion as illustrative of the impact of populist-right nastiness on major political parties. Hewson might also have cited the Trump-like comments of Immigration Minister Peter Dutton in *The Daily*

Telegraph on 1 November 2018, that those asylum seekers on Nauru who didn't go to the USA are not 'genuine refugees' and that 'reports have come back to people on Nauru that it's all a bit financially tight there because you have to get a job and because there's no welfare there'. Naturally Dutton presented no hard evidence to back up his slur.

Once it is accepted that the toxicity of the populist right is becoming deeply embedded in the value system of Australian political and public discourse, the issue is how to reassert liberal values and why it is important to do so.

The liberal values of tolerance, free choice, openness, and a preparedness to act generously towards those who seek shelter in this wealthy land and to conduct ourselves as decent international citizens are worth pursuing and enforcing for many reasons, but the one that is readily apparent is the need to begin to heal the divisions that are so evident in Australia today.

The 'culture wars', the constant demonising of 'The Other', the arsenal of populist-right weaponry misused by politicians and the media to distort and lie … all of this is corrosive of a liberal democracy.

Michael Ignatieff, the Canadian intellectual and former leader of that genuinely liberal nation's Liberal Party, presciently observed some five years ago that for 'democracies to work, politicians need to respect the difference between an enemy and an adversary'. 'An adversary', Ignatieff observed, 'is someone you want to defeat. An enemy is someone you have to destroy. With adversaries, compromise is honorable: Today's adversary could be tomorrow's ally. With enemies, on the other hand, compromise is appeasement.'

And Ignatieff might have been talking about politicians like Howard and Dutton and those who support them when he observed that politicians (in this context in the USA):

> ratchet up manageable differences of policy into conflicts over identity and value. In this way, what Freud called the 'narcissism of minor differences' drives party activists into closed worlds of discourse, while leaving the rest of Americans feeling that 'the system' fails to serve them at all. They cease participating altogether, leaving the politicians to brawl in a deserted public square.[9]

Ignatieff's words aptly describe Australia today. Too much is now viewed as an existential battle. Xenophobia and other irrational fears are the order of the day. Politicians and media scream about 'African gangs' and about boats of desperate asylum seekers appearing on the horizon and striking fear into the heart of Australians; that there are 'cultural Marxists' determined to corrupt our children; that the national broadcaster is out of control as a vehicle for leftist ranting; and yes, devious Marxists are trying to bring down the capitalist system.

In the parliaments across the nation – but let's focus on Canberra – this fracturing of Australia resulting from the decline of liberal values leads to the election of white supremacists like Fraser Anning (whose first speech to parliament in August 2018 made the 'rivers of blood' speech of British MP Enoch Powell look like a treatise on tolerance), Pauline Hanson, and misogynists like David Leyonhjelm or law-and-order populists like Derryn Hinch. And on it goes.

It is said that the rise of the populist right is because the 'elites' have not listened to the 'battlers' or 'ordinary Australians'. This statement, or observation, is inherently problematic because it divides Australian from Australian. It makes enemies of the 'elites' and 'the ordinary Australian' the friend that every politician and populist media commentator wants to embrace. The 'elites' are 'condescending towards the views of "ordinary people",' says *The Australian*'s columnist Judith Sloan.

Those individuals who believe in liberal immigration policies, who are not wedded to Western civilisation triumphalism, who do not believe in nationalism and who support strong human rights measures and culture are termed 'elites'. They are 'out of touch', it is said, with 'ordinary people'. But this is a lazy populist-right narrative and nothing more.

Reclaiming liberal values

In a society in which liberal values prevail, there is a welcoming of divergent points of view. Simply because a person has post-graduate qualifications, or works in global markets, or lives in an inner suburb of a city and votes Greens or left independent, does not make them 'elite'. Nor does it make their voice any less worthwhile than the voice of the farmer, the tradesperson, the part-time retail worker or an individual existing on a disability pension. And one could say vice versa.

But equally, in a society underpinned by liberal values, there is no monopoly on truth or wisdom. There is not, as is often the case with the populist right, this idea that simply because there is strong support among 'ordinary Australians' (which is often code for marginal seats) for a particular populist policy (such as harsh treatment of asylum seekers both on- and offshore) or for punitive measures (such as aspects of anti-terror laws or industrial-scale jailing of the marginalised and mentally unwell), then the policy must be right.

Good policy, as in policy aimed at outcomes that enhance the welfare of society and the democratic values underpinning it, is not always policy that is populist. Too often the populist right makes noise through its favoured media outlets, and then what emerges is 'policy on the run' from politicians desperate to curry favour with those they see as representing 'ordinary Australians'. This is why, for example, some jurisdictions like Victoria are squandering billions of dollars on ramping up criminal laws and punishments when it is clear that such a response is not based on any evidence that shows that it works.

If we are to blunt the populist right, we must plead with politicians, media and interest groups to consider the long-term consequences for decisions taken today that are antithetical to fairness and decency. As demonstrated by the Stolen Generations and the policy of forced adoption of children born to single mothers in the not-so-distant past, these types of 'popular' policies built on prejudice (and racism in the case of the Stolen Generations) lead to intergenerational suffering and dispossession.

There is no doubt that our society will pay a substantial price, one day in the decades to come, for the cruelty meted out to asylum seekers. That Australia has so readily embraced the populist-right politics of nationalism and xenophobia perpetuated by former prime minister John Howard in the 2001 Tampa incident and beyond will be seen as a great error.

There will be an apology and there will be, as there already has been, massive compensation to pay. The damage done internationally to Australia's reputation as a genuinely liberal and therefore fair society by the pursuit of extraordinary cruelty towards men, women and children in immigration detention centres will take some years to redress, and in the future there will be a prime minister and a government that will say to the international community that it will not happen again.

The issue of immigration, together with that of refugees, is an example of the sort of policy discussion that could look so different, and so much more rational and compassionate, if we utilised the framework of liberal values instead of the populist-right settings on which both coalition parties and the ALP have built their politics since 2001. A policy discussion based on liberal values would assure Australians that border security does matter yet is not an either/or proposition, that immigration policy has to be informed by values such as fairness, equal treatment, global responsibility, and balancing the interests of sovereignty with the advantages that come to Australia from migration. This would be a policy whereby cruelty and unjustifiable hardship, such as inflicting destitution on asylum seekers, have no place because they are counterproductive and, more importantly, utterly inconsistent with liberal values.

We Australians could also surely have discussions about the emerging issues of gender and sexuality without the hysteria presented by the populist right – a debate informed by the fact that, in a society where liberal values have pride of place, there is an acceptance that cultural mores and norms are not static, that organised religion does not – and should not – exercise disproportionate influence in moral and cultural debates because secular beliefs are equally important for us to heed.

As John Hewson warns us and as Michael Ignatieff bleakly describes, ensuring that Australia does not continue to head down the road taken in parts of Europe and in the USA under President Trump requires leadership by the political class, and this includes the media. Pandering to prejudice and fear, and reinforcing a false sense of danger for those who believe themselves to be threatened existentially by 'The Other', is easy; it is the populist right's modus operandi. But it leads to ever more extreme statements, actions and political gestures.

Last word

It seems that there is no territory the populist right will not touch; outrage is in its DNA. The former racial discrimination commissioner, Dr Tim Soutphommasane, a whipping boy for the populist right, described it this way in a speech delivered at Sydney University on 19 July 2018:

> You think of what we're seeing as regular features of public discussion today as well. Once, perhaps twice, a week on breakfast television you are seeing Pauline Hanson and others be part of not just the debate but of the agenda setting of our debate.
>
> And then there are calls for the banning of the burqa or the niqab; calls for the banning of Muslim immigration. There was even a call recently for the mass internment of Muslims by Jim Molan, a senator. These are just some

examples of the kind of discourse that you're seeing normalised now.

Another example that Soutphommasane referred to was of a Channel 7 *Sunrise* commentator, Prue MacSween, saying 'that if she saw the commentator Yassmin Abdel-Magied on the street she would be inclined to run her over'. Soutphommasane lamented that 'this nationalist, populist style of politics' is 'gaining some currency'. He is right.

Perhaps the most important reason to oppose vigorously the rise of the populist right is that it represents a grab for power and an exercise in paternalism. The populist-right tactics of division, conflict and manufactured outrage are designed to cower the political class, or at least those it has not captured or who are not its representatives already. Far from wanting an accommodation of views, the populist right wants to order the ABC around, to threaten journalists and editors who do not meet its criteria or its loyalty and adherence to conservative views. The populist right is not interested in dialogue about human rights, discrimination laws and what it calls identity politics. All of these are impediments to the carte blanche it wants to use to exercise freedom of its speech and its ideas.

The populist right of course has the right to be heard. Freedom of speech and thought is critical to a well-functioning, liberal democracy. But there is a world of difference between, on the one hand, being heard, and, on the other, injecting ideas into discourse in a manner that is respectful of others and is mindful that there is no monopoly on truth or what is deemed to be the best for a society.

Notes

Chapter 1 The Decline of Liberal Values: Is Australia any Different?

1 A term often used in reference to trade wars, 'zero sum' originates in game theory, where one party's gain is equivalent to another's loss, so the net result is always zero.

2 Rob D Kaiser and Michael McGuire (29 April 1999) 'Blair Unveils Bold Intervention Doctrine', *Chicago Tribune*. https://www.chicagotribune.com/news/ct-xpm-1999-04-23-9904230097-story.html

3 Jonathan Chait (27 January 2015) 'Not a Very PC Thing to Say', *New York Magazine*. http://nymag.com/daily/intelligencer/2015/01/not-a-very-pc-thing-to-say.html

4 Museum of Australian Democracy (2018) 'Defining Democracy'. https://www.moadoph.gov.au/democracy/defining-democracy/

5 Edward Luce (2017) *The Retreat of Western Liberalism*, United Kingdom: Little Brown, p. 204.

6 Karl Popper (2011) *The Open Society and Its Enemies*, United Kingdom: Taylor and Francis Ltd, p. 35.

Chapter 2 Tracing the Decline: Hanson, Tampa and 9/11

1 Pauline Hanson (10 September 1996) *House of Representatives Hansard*, p. 3859.

2 Paul Karp (7 July 2016) 'Pauline Hanson Should Not be a "Scorned Species", John Howard says', *The Guardian*. https://www.theguardian.com/australia-news/2016/jul/07/pauline-hanson-should-not-be-a-scorned-species-john-howard-says

3 National Museum of Australia (2018) 'Defining moments in Australian history: the Tampa incident'. http://www.nma.gov.au/online_features/defining_moments/featured/tampa_affair
4 Kim Beazley (29 August 2001) *House of Representatives Hansard*, p. 30570.
5 Don Rothwell (2002) 'The Law of the Sea and the MV Tampa Incident: Reconciling Maritime Principles with Coastal State Sovereignty', *Public Law Review*, Vol 13, p. 127.
6 Professor Krygier is a member of the School of Law at UNSW. http://www.law.unsw.edu.au/news/2015/08/rule-law-what-it-why-it-matters-and-what-threatens-it
7 Hannah Arendt (2007) *Between Past and Future: Eight Exercises in Political Thought*, New York, Penguin Books, p. 252.
8 Parliament of Australia (2002) 'Senate Committee Report on A Certain Maritime Incident'.
9 George Williams (2011) 'A Decade of Australian Anti-Terror Laws', *Melbourne University Law Review*, Vol 35, p. 1138.
10 As above, p. 1145
11 Jeffrey C Isaac (2004) 'Social Science and Liberal Values in a Time of War', *Perspectives on Politics*, Vol 2, Issue 3, pp. 475–83.

Chapter 3 The Tools of Populism: Elites, Ordinary Australians, 'The Other'

1 Richard Pithouse (7 September 2018) 'The Migrant and the Enemy Within', *Mail and Guardian*. https://mg.co.za/article/2018-09-07-00-the-migrant-and-the-enemy-within
2 Viktor Orbán (28 July 2018) 'Every Country has the Right to Reject Immigration', *Website of the Hungarian Government*. http://www.kormany.hu/en/the-prime-minister/news/every-country-has-the-right-to-reject-immigration
3 Michael Koziol (15 December 2016) 'Peter Dutton Calls for Pro-Christmas Uprising Against "Political Correctness Gone Mad"', *Sydney Morning Herald*. https://www.smh.com.au/politics/federal/peter-dutton-calls-for-prochristmas-uprising-against-political-correctness-gone-mad-20161215-gtbj63.html
4 Kevin Donnelly (5 May 2018) 'Australia Under Attack from Political Correctness', *The Spectator*. https://www.spectator.co.uk/2018/05/australia-under-attack-from-political-correctness/

5 Stephen Chavura (31 August 2018) 'Free Speech is Scott Morrison's Chance to Lead like Menzies', *The Australian.*
6 Melissa Fyffe (18 August 2017) 'Yassmin Abdel-Magied on Becoming "Australia's Most Publicly Hated Muslim"', *Sydney Morning Herald.* https://www.smh.com.au/lifestyle/yassmin-abdelmagied-on-becoming-australias-most-publicly-hated-muslim-20170816-gxxb7d.html
7 Naomi Klein (2 June 2016) 'Let Them Drown – The Violence of Othering in a Warming World', *London Review of Books,* Vol 38, No 11, p. 11.
8 John Budarick (1 August 2018) 'Why the Media are to Blame for Racialising Melbourne's "African Gang" Problem', *The Conversation.* https://theconversation.com/why-the-media-are-to-blame-for-racialising-melbournes-african-gang-problem-100761
9 Roland Bleiker, David Campbell, Emma Hutchison and Xzarina Nicholson (11 December 2013) 'The Visual Dehumanisation of Refugees', *Australian Journal of Political Science,* Vol 48, No 4, p. 398.
10 Binoy Kampmark (4 August 2017) 'The Long Crucifixion of Gillian Triggs', *Independent Australia.* https://independentaustralia.net/life/life-display/gillian-triggs-human-rights-and-ideology,10573

Chapter 4 Kill all the Judges: Decline of the Rule of Law

1 Paul Karp (22 June 2018) 'Three Federal Ministers to Apologise to Victorian Court to Avert Possible Contempt Charges', *The Guardian.* https://www.theguardian.com/australia-news/2017/jun/22/three-federal-ministers-to-apologise-to-victorian-court-to-avert-possible-contempt-charges
2 Tom Bingham (16 November 2006) 'The Rule of Law', lecture given at the Centre for Public Law, *Cambridge University.* https://www.cpl.law.cam.ac.uk/sir-david-williams-lectures2006-rule-law/rule-law-text-transcript
3 Tom Bingham (2011) *The Rule of Law,* London, Penguin Books, p. 5.
4 Rob D Kaiser and Michael McGuire (29 April 1999) 'Blair Unveils Bold Intervention Doctrine', *Chicago Tribune.* https://www.chicagotribune.com/news/ct-xpm-1999-04-23-9904230097-story.html

5 Tom Bingham (2011) *The Rule of Law*, London, Penguin Books, p. 8.
6 Tom Bingham (16 November 2006) 'The Rule of Law', lecture given at the Centre for Public Law, *Cambridge University*. and Tom Bingham (2011) *The Rule of Law*, London, Penguin Books, pp. 48–54.
7 Parliament of Tasmania (30 August 2018) House of Assembly Hansard. http://www.parliament.tas.gov.au/ParliamentSearch/isysquery/d51192d5-0d00-4ab1-85f2-fe8f6631f787/1/doc/#term0_1
8 Tom Bingham (2011) *The Rule of Law*, London, Penguin Books, p. 55.
9 As above, p. 68.
10 As above, pp. 66–94.
11 Philip Alston (1 February 2017) 'The Populist Challenge to Human Rights', *Journal of Human Rights Practice*, Vol 9, Issue 1, pp. 1–15.
12 James Allan (24 June 2018) 'Australia Explained to Hungarians', *Quadrant*. https://quadrant.org.au/opinion/qed/2018/06/australia-explained-hungarians/
13 Tom Bingham (16 November 2006) 'The Rule of Law', lecture given at the Centre for Public Law, *Cambridge University* and Tom Bingham (2011) *The Rule of Law*, London, Penguin Books, p. 151.
14 As above.
15 Kaldor Centre (23 May 2016) 'Refugees with an Adverse Security Assessment by ASIO'. http://www.kaldorcentre.unsw.edu.au/publication/refugees-adverse-security-assessment-asio
16 Tom Bingham (16 November 2006) 'The Rule of Law', lecture given at the Centre for Public Law, *Cambridge University*.
17 Janet Albrechtsen (June 2002) 'National Interest Versus International Law: The International Criminal Court', *The Samuel Griffith Society*. http://www.samuelgriffith.org.au/papers/html/volume14/v14chap10.html

Chapter 5 The Rise of the Right, Personified

1 Ashley Middleton (2016) 'Populist Radical Right Parties and the Securitization of Migration in France', *Independent Study Project (ISP)*, Collection 2430, pp. 10–11.

2 Cynthia Wong (21 September 2018) 'Turning Our Technology Against Us', *The Strategist.*
3 Mats Ekström, Marianna Patrona and Joanna Thornborrow (2018) 'Right-wing Populism and the Dynamics of Style: A Discourse-analytic Perspective on Mediated Political Performances', *Palgrave Communications,* Vol 4, Issue 1, p. 83.
4 Mike Pezzullo (13 October 2017) speech to the Trans-Tasman Business Circle. https://soundcloud.com/the-mandarin-816831024/full-speech-michael-pezzullo-on-the-department-of-home-affairs
5 Joseph Burgo, (13 March 2013) 'The Emotional Psychology of a Two-party System', *The Atlantic.*
6 John Keane (29 September 2017) 'The Pathologies of Populism', *The Conversation.* https://theconversation.com/the-pathologies-of-populism-82593
7 The Papua New Guinea Supreme Court, in a decision on 26 April 2016, found that the detainees at Manus Island had been falsely imprisoned by Australia and PNG.
8 Andrew Arato (25 April 2017) 'Populism and the Courts', *Verfassungsblog.* https://verfassungsblog.de/populism-and-the-courts/
9 Stan Grant (25 August 2018) 'Liberal Party's Civil War Isn't Over – It's Part of a Global Battle', *ABC online.* https://www.abc.net.au/news/2018-08-25/liberal-party-civil-war-isnt-over/10162424
10 James McDougall (16 November 2016) 'No, This Isn't the 1930s – But Yes, This is Fascism', *The Conversation.* https://theconversation.com/no-this-isnt-the-1930s-but-yes-this-is-fascism-68867

Chapter 6 The Real Danger of the Populist Right

1 Simeon Thomas-Wilson (20 June 2017) 'National Support for Hobart City Council's Australia Day Date Change Push', *The Mercury.* https://www.themercury.com.au/news/politics/national-support-for-hobart-city-councils-australia-day-date-change-push/news-story/a17375a510ea6eaa44b198cbcb16b32e
2 Renee Viellaris (15 August 2017) 'Australia Day: Local Councils Warned Not to Politicise Citizenship Ceremonies', *The Courier Mail.*

3 Felicity Caldwell (12 December 2017) 'Councillor Could Have Citizenship Ceremony Powers Revoked After Comments', *Brisbane Times*. https://www.brisbanetimes.com.au/politics/queensland/councillor-asked-to-explain-or-his-citizenship-ceremony-powers-could-be-revoked-20171212-p4yxn8.html
4 Tony Walker (11 June 2018) 'In Australia's Relentless Culture Wars: Tony Abbott Strikes Again', *Sydney Morning Herald*. https://www.smh.com.au/education/in-australia-s-relentless-culture-wars-tony-abbott-strikes-again-20180608-p4zkbu.html
5 Michelle Grattan (18 June 2018) 'The Threat to the ABC is Not sale But More Bullying', *ABC online*. https://www.abc.net.au/news/2018-06-18/threat-to-the-abc-is-not-sale-but-more-bullying/9879420
6 Peter Bloom (11 August 2018) 'Populists on Both Left and Right Claim to be Fighting for "The People" – But Who Exactly are They?', *The Independent*. https://www.independent.co.uk/voices/democracy-left-wing-right-wing-will-great-british-people-populism-a8487346.html
7 Piers Akerman (9 September 2018) 'Scott Morrison Channels Robert Menzies' Family Values', *The Daily Telegraph*.
8 Francis Fukuyama (September – October 2018) 'Against Identity Politics: The New Tribalism and the Crisis of Democracy', *Foreign Affairs*. https://www.foreignaffairs.com/articles/americas/2018-08-14/against-identity-politics-tribalism-francis-fukuyama
9 Michael Ignatieff (16 October 2013) 'Enemies vs. Adversaries', *The New York Times*. https://www.nytimes.com/2013/10/17/opinion/enemies-vs-adversaries.html